Cancer of the Spirit

of the

a novel by Ife

VIP Publishing, Inc.

VIP Publishing, Inc.

ISBN 0-9748136-0-5
Library of Congress: 2003116838

Printed in the United States of America
First Printing
April 2004

Editor: Janet Overton
Jacket and Text Design: Kyle Design Group, Inc., 2004
info@kyledesigngroup.com
SootheOurSouls.com Website Development & Design, and
Soothe Our Souls Logo Design: Mumbosauce Multimedia, 2004
www.mumbosauce.com
Book Jacket Photograpy: Workbook Stock, 2004
Website Models: Corbis Images, 2004
Contact Author at: Ife@SootheOurSouls.com
or www.SootheOurSouls.com
or
Soothe Our Souls
9900 Greenbelt Road, Suite E 212
Lanham, MD 20706-2264

Cancer
of
the
Spirit

a novel by Ife

VIP Publishing, Inc.

Dedications

*T*o my ninety-three year old mother, Johnnie Mae Humbert Kilgore, and my father, Wells Herbert Lee Kilgore, who joined our ancestors on August 8, 1992, thanks for all of your loving care and numerous struggles that have made your three daughters—Carole (known as Ife), Cynthia, and Brenda—who we are today.

Mom and Daddy's 50th Wedding Anniversary Celebration

To the most recent blessings in my life—my grandchildren. Nandi Anika Carson, my granddaughter, who was four months old when I seriously began writing Cancer of the Spirit, and my grandson, Khalid Valentine Keene, II, words can never express what you mean to your 'G'. Thanks to both of you and Stefan, Demond and Cori, my other "Grands," for the abundance of joy you have brought me in such a short time. I'm looking forward to so much more.

Cancer of the Spirit Contents

Acknowledgments

From the depth of my heart, I would like to express my gratitude to Bill 'Damani' Keene, the wonderful father of our three children and the best husband a woman could have, for the sincere and loving support that he always gives me in every area of my life. Our thirty-eight year marriage has always been a true partnership, and was no different while I was writing this book. His initial editing of *Cancer of the Spirit* is very much appreciated. I love you, Booby!

A special thank you to our two sons, Khalid and Malik, and our daughter Kweli, who, like my husband, have always encouraged me to pursue my dreams. Our three children are each a true blessing. My husband and I sometimes rhetorically remark, "What did we do to deserve them?" We are so proud to be their parents.

I want to express my sincere appreciation to my entire extended family and all of the friends who supported the writing of this book. They, like other readers, may see themselves somewhere in the pages of *Cancer of the Spirit.*

I particularly thank my cousins Barbara and Jim Carney, and my brother-in-law Gary Brown, for the invaluable information they shared with me on writing, publishing, publishers, and literary agents. Their enthusiastic support of this project will never be forgotten.

I want to graciously thank Dr. Marcus Reginald Carson, Dr. Kweli Keene Carson, Rev. Dr. James Coleman, Gregory and Shirlene James, Asha Brown, Dennis Brown, Grace Wiggins-Schauer, and Ansa Tyus for taking time to read all, or portions, of *Cancer of the Spirit*, and make valuable comments.

I would like to personally acknowledge individuals like Iyanla Vanzant and Oprah Winfrey, who consistently encourage and challenge women to step out of their boxes and to be true to themselves.

Thanks to the Sisterspace and Books in Washington, DC for the excellent information I received while participating in their writers workshops.

A special thank you to Kwame Alexander, poet, playwright, producer and publishing consultant, for providing writers with an opportunity to self-publish. His "Do the Write Thing Boot Camp" armed me with the knowledge and tools necessary to successfully complete *Cancer of the Spirit*, a project I began over four years ago.

To my fantastic sister, Brenda Brown, thanks for the numerous hours you spent editing *Cancer of the Spirit* after the initial writing and during the proofreading phase. Your priceless suggestions and editorial input helped the book come to light.

Lastly, I would like to thank my most competent, dedicated and "beyond-the-call-of-duty" editor, Janet Overton. Her devotion to the project, expertise, suggestions for character development and attention to details have given a wonderful depth and beautiful texture to this, my first book. For this, she has my eternal respect and gratitude. Thank you, Janet.

Author's Note

*C*ancer of the Spirit is truly a labor of love, as well as a reflection of my chosen name, Ifetayo, which means "love brings happiness." I chose this name more than twenty-five years ago because it was then, and still remains, a true reflection of my life. Ife, a derivative of Ifetayo, simply means "love".

This novel portrays the day-to-day struggles of ten women who have experienced varying degrees of "cancer of the spirit." Each of their stories will take you on a journey—one that will be painfully familiar to some, unique to some, and maybe an unexpected blessing to others. The women's searching for answers to self-imposed and other questions; their growing love for themselves, and their acceptance of personal empowerment and self-respect, were catalysts for their respective recoveries or self-insight.

Cancer of the Spirit gives me an opportunity to reach a large audience—one that can relate to the challenges that one or more of the characters encounter. Each chapter has been developed with the intent to spark self-examination and offer to those in a state of despair, the courage to initiate action.

For whatever amount of discomfort the reading of *Cancer of the Spirit* may provoke, I am certain that you will also experience feelings of joy, renewal, empowerment and awareness.

I hope these stories will create a sense of intimacy between you and each character, especially those whose issues resonate with your life experience. To my male readers, this book will be beneficial in helping you relate to and understand many of the innermost feelings of the women in your life. Read it with an open mind, especially if a woman in your life gave it to you.

Thanks so much for reading *Cancer of the Spirit*. I appreciate your support. With much love. Ife

Chapter One

The Get Together
Houston, Texas

Ama Campbell lovingly shakes out and then floats the embroidered fuchsia tablecloth over and onto the sturdy old mahogany dining room table. Patting it smooth, she is conscious, as always, of the generations of ancestors who graced its boards. Her mother, Kay, deceased now for seventeen years, had passed on her love of this table to Ama long before it was entrusted to her care. The doorbell's ring jolts her from daydreaming. "Oh, my God! Is it four o'clock already?" She rushes through the kitchen toward the front door, glancing at the clock on the stove as she passes by and sighs with relief, "Thank goodness, it's only three fifteen." She opens the door and there stands Tommy, the handsome brother from the flower shop.

"Hey, Ama, what's up? Why all the flowers? You got something special going on?" he asks as he hands her two of the three pink and white stargazer lily arrangements she ordered.

Excited, she responds, "I'm having a get together this weekend for a few of my mother's and my friends. It's in honor of her memory and to celebrate the upcoming kick-off of my program for at-risk youth—something I've been planning for several years now."

"Wow, that's really cool, Ama. Congratulations. I wish I could come." As he goes to the truck to get the third arrangement, Ama shouts, "It's a women-only thang." Then adds with a grin, when he returns, "Maybe next time." But as she closes the door on his departing back, enjoying first the view of his walk, and then the look and fragrance of the blossoms she carries, she thinks to herself, "These flowers are absolutely gorgeous, just like that fine brother-man. I'm gonna have something—anything—to invite him to. He's real easy on the eyes."

Ama quickly refocuses on preparing for the get together as she scans the living room to decide where to place the flowers, and subconsciously notes the seating arrangements. She wonders how many of the twenty invited women—ten of her mother's friends, and ten of her own—will actually show up. Several are coming from out of town. She assumes that those staying for the weekend have already checked into the nearby hotel that she recommended. She feels guilty about not checking on them, but has spent every minute preparing for this very special occasion. Ena is the only one staying with her.

Ama wants everything to be perfect for what she imagines will be one of the most memorable evenings of her life. She reflects on how proud her mother would be of her and thinks that Ma would have planned just such a special event to celebrate this major accomplishment in her life. She inhales deeply.

Every inch of her small two-bedroom home is filled with heavenly aromas. The homemade rolls dominate, but are forgotten as her eyes turn to the small folding table and card table. She mumbles, "Where the hell did I put those tablecloths?" Just as the doorbell rings, she remembers that they're in the side compartment of the buffet, behind the tall ice-tea glasses. This time when she opens the door, it's her first guest, her friend, Makeba, dressed regally in a fabulous black and white mud-cloth outfit—with matching hat—looking like a real African princess. With genuine joy Ama says, "It is just like you to show up first, even though you came all the way from L.A. Even when you're early, you're always right on time." They hug—their arms letting each other know how much each has been missed. Ama says, "Girl, I knew you would be the first one here; you are just too punctual." They both laugh as they enter the living room.

"It's hard to believe I've let so much time go by without seeing you," Makeba says to Ama.

"I know what you mean, girl," Ama sighs. The two friends had hit it off immediately when they met ten years before while Ama's family was in Los Angeles on vacation. Kay was an ex-girlfriend of Makeba's boyfriend's Uncle Joe. Through the years Kay and Joe had remained good friends, as had Ama and Makeba. But these friends have only minutes to catch up before other guests begin arriving.

Marlana, Kay's friend, is the second to arrive with a much older woman whom Ama doesn't recognize. Ama was a teenager when Marlana visited Kay in Morristown, New Jersey. As young girls in Philadelphia, Kay and Marlana had attended the same church, sang in the choir, and were "saved" around the same time. Over time, Kay moved to Morristown, and Marlana to Wilmington, Delaware, but they had stayed in touch throughout the years. Now it was Ama's time to renew the friendship.

"Auntie Marlana!" Ama greets her warmly. "Do you still want me to call you that?"

Ife

Marlana smiles, "I most certainly do. And I want you to meet my Aunt Hattie Mae, who wanted to come and join the festivities."

"It's my pleasure to meet you. I'm glad you came with Auntie Marlana," Ama says.

As she guides them toward the living room, Marlana whispers to Ama, "At the last minute, Aunt Hattie Mae decided to come. I was relieved because I don't like leaving her at home alone. She's a little feeble now."

Ama introduces the newcomers to Makeba and they're all getting resettled and acquainted when Ena makes a grand entrance, looking as if she's just stepped off the stage of the Ebony Fashion Show. Wearing the classic short black dress that hugs her tall shapely body, she is enviably together from head to toe. She knows it too. Ama can't help but comment on how good Ena looks.

Ena, on the other hand, enters with, "Dag, Ama, it's hot as hell in Houston!" while fanning herself with her hand. "Not good for keeping my make-up together. And carrying this heavy bag ain't helping either."

As Ama closes the door behind Ena, she says, "Girl, that little bit of sweat ain't gonna hurt you none. Besides, there's nobody here for you to impress anyhow. This is a *women's* gathering." Laughing together, they go into the living room and greet the other women as Ama introduces Ena.

Ama and Ena first met at their sorority's annual National Convention two years earlier. Despite Ena being nearly ten years younger, Ama noticed that Ena exuded confidence and she admired that about her. Ena, on the other hand, was impressed with Ama's kindness toward others. Ama was always the first one to offer a helping hand to a soror in need. They became fast friends at that convention and have remained so ever since. Ama has only a moment to sit and sip some iced tea when the doorbell rings again.

This time, she opens the door to Dominique. They both hesitate a moment before speaking.

"Hello, Ama. It's wonderful to see you again. It must be seventeen years since we've seen each other. You're a lovely young lady."

"Thanks Miss Dominique" Ama says after a moment's pause, "I'm so happy that you've come. Please come in."

Stepping in cautiously, Dominique says, "I'm so pleased you invited me. I wouldn't have dreamed of not coming. Your mother was one of the kindest, most genuine people I've ever met." As Dominique crosses into the living room, the other women's surprise at seeing a white woman enter is evident by the abrupt cessation of what had been a lively conversation and by the looks on some of their faces. Ama says to the other ladies, "I'd like you to meet Miss Dominique. She and Ma became friends many years ago. Ma worked with her husband, Mr. Jerome." Dominique continues, "Although Kay worked with my husband, she and I became friends when we discovered that both of us had family in Marshall, VA. My grandparents were born and raised there and, much to my surprise, Kay spent several summers there with aunts and uncles. Those ties ignited a lasting friendship between us."

The doorbell rings again. As Ama excuses herself, she whispers to Dominique, "I'm really happy that you're here."

Catherine, to celebrate the way she met Kay, comes in tastefully made up and beautifully coiffed. She hands Ama a fancy gift bag full of every imaginable make-up item. Catherine had met Kay while shop-

5

ping in Manhattan. She accidentally bumped into Kay at the cosmetics counter causing her to drop and break a bottle of foundation. To make up for her clumsiness, Catherine invited Kay to lunch. They became friends and had many fun-filled shopping sprees and lunches together.

When Ama opens the bag, she says, "Wow, I probably couldn't use all of this makeup in a lifetime. I won't ever have to buy any again. Thanks very much Miss Catherine. Oh, there's the doorbell again."

As soon as Ama opens the door, she knows immediately who the new arrival is even though she'd never met her. Kay had always described Alicia (Leesha) as a homely woman and a real live wire. Ama knows this is Leesha because she has remained true to that description. Moving towards Ama, Leesha says, "Hey, baby, can I get a big hug?"

Leesha and Kay met at a national AME Church conference twenty-five years ago. They bonded right away and corresponded and called often between conferences. As soon as Leesha struts into the living room, Ama sees that Leesha may prove to be the "livest" wire at this gathering too. Leesha's comical description of her headaches in traffic soon has everyone laughing so hard that Sharon's quiet entrance goes almost unnoticed.

Ama had extricated herself from the laughing circle around Leesha at the sound of the doorbell. Sharon often described her initial connection to Kay as a somewhat supernatural experience. She had a dream about meeting a girl in a restaurant who would become a lifelong friend. The dream became reality when she met Kay in Hal's Restaurant on Georgia Avenue, across the street from D.C. Teachers College, where both of them were studying for finals over greasy cheeseburgers and making do with the one and only napkin that Hal was notorious for giving. Because Kay attended D.C. Teachers, which didn't have dormitories, she lived "in the city." Sharon, whose alma mater is Howard University, lived on campus and graciously offered Kay a place to study. A lasting friendship emerged.

Shortly after Sharon is introduced, gets a cool drink, and takes the last space on the sofa, Ama asks, "Miss Sharon, have you had any more good dreams come true lately? If you have, I certainly hope I was in one of them. Ma told me the story several times about your reaction to meeting her. She said you thought it was 'a dream come true'."

"I've had many more good dreams, Ama, but none that have come true—I'm sorry to say."

Helen, another of Kay's friends from her days as a student at D.C. Teachers, saunters in not looking a day over forty. Ama greets her lovingly and gets a chair from the dining room for her.

Kay was a senior, Helen a freshman, when they met. During the year they were in school together, Kay became a mentor to Helen. After Kay graduated, Helen stayed in touch, never forgetting the positive impact Kay had on her. After introducing her to the other women, Ama reminds Helen, "You knew my mother longer than anyone else here—including me."

After a while, as everyone is having a great time and enjoying the food, Ama announces, "Well, I guess no one else will be arriving. I invited a few others." Helen promptly adds, "With everything that's going on in my life, I almost didn't make it myself." The noisy, melodic and fun-filled mood suddenly shifts to a solemn ambiance. It is very evident that the women have become very comfortable with each other during this short time when Helen, finishing her sweet potato pie and continuing to sip iced tea, begins offering an absorbing and painful unfolding of events in her life. At first she had been talking to Leesha and Makeba, but when some of the others overheard a reference to Kay, they fell silent and began to listen in.

The afternoon transforms into evening. The extending shadows outside blend into one darkening landscape and become a metaphor for ten women sharing their lives. Surprisingly, all of them are drawn into a stream of converging consciousness. Each woman follows Helen's lead and tells her own story throughout a long evening that flows into an even longer night—and an emotion-filled weekend.

Chapter Two

Helen
Age: 51 - Washington, DC

Helen begins, "Ama, this was such a wonderful idea—to gather your mother's friends and your friends here tonight to commemorate her life and to celebrate your recent accomplishment."

The ladies chime in with, "Hear, hear," and, "Right on, sister!"

"Miss Helen," interjects Ama, "Would you mind if I tape you? From what Ma told me, you knew her well and you've led a remarkable life."

"Ama, that's fine with me." Helen continues, "Thinking about your mother reminds me of what a source of strength and comfort she was for me during my younger years. Some of you may know that Kay was a mentor to me during my first year at D.C. Teachers College, my first year away from home and on my own. That year I stopped being a child and began being a woman, and Kay was a sheltering Rock of Gibraltar. I dearly miss her. Enjoying the company of all of you reminds me of the importance of this kind of companionship, this kind of support. I must tell you, it has been such a Godsend to me recently—the friendship of women. During the past year my life has taken so many twists and turns."

Ama asks, "Is it something you'd be willing to share with us? I, for one, would really like to hear more about the life of someone who knew my mother so well."

Well, if it's all right with you ladies, I will share my story with you. But things I've discovered about myself recently make me feel the importance of starting at the beginning, my first memory. And what I first, most vividly remember is the day my Daddy left us, even though I was only four years old. Helen takes a deep breath, exhales and then begins to speak in a quiet but confident voice.

The day was as gloomy as the expression on Ma's face when Daddy closed the door behind him. He had always been the stabilizing force in our family. But I guess he grew tired of taking care of Ma and almost single-handedly raising Ellen and me. Ellen was my twin sister. His role was both mother and father from the day we were born, Ma being a nonfunctioning alcoholic. So I guess he decided just not to do it anymore. At least that is what I told myself for many years after he left. I think I still subconsciously blame Ma for Daddy leaving. She couldn't even keep a job or do the basic things required to take care of Ellen and me, or our home. Daddy was passionately protective of our mother and us—"his little girls".

Ellen and I were devastated by his sudden disappearance. Our hearts were thoroughly broken. For at least a year, we cried ourselves to sleep every night. Ellen wasn't as outgoing as I was. She didn't take to people outside our family very well. But that was forty-seven years ago. Ellen died recently of digestive and intestinal problems. She struggled for years with bulimia and other eating disorders. I don't think she ever got over Daddy leaving. As she got older, she used food to comfort her aching, to fill the void. At first, she seemed to embrace food like a lover; but ultimately she came to treat it like an enemy— making herself vomit, rejecting food as though she were rejecting a lover who betrayed her. By the time she died, she was literally skin and bones. I still hurt so badly from losing her. I miss her so much.

When Daddy first left, Ma assured us that he would be back. But after a while, even at that young age, we somehow sensed that her belief in his impending return sprang more from her bottle of gin than from reality. After a couple of months, Ma rarely spoke about him. She tried to take over running the house, but just couldn't; and we were basically caring for ourselves as best we could—at four years old. But it was obvious that we weren't eating properly or being taken care of at all. Two of Ma's sisters, Aunt Marjorie and Aunt Lynn, offered to take Ellen and me temporarily while Ma got help for her drinking. Although they had children of their own, they were willing to keep us. Ma refused their offer. I later learned that there had been a series of family feuds between them and Ma. What those feuds were about, I still don't truly know. What I do know is that my aunts eventually reported Ma to the state.

When the officials from child welfare showed up to take Ellen and me away, Ma became very hostile. She yelled, "Get the hell out of my house; you're not going to take my babies anywhere. I'll be damned if they're going to anybody's foster home. I'll give them up for adoption before that happens." Luckily, she was sober the day they came. I'll never forget the tears streaming from her eyes and the sadness in her voice that day. I believe her fear and anger were the result of her own experience as a child—being tossed from one foster home to another. I can still hear her screaming, "You can forget it if you think my baby girls are going through that!" She wasn't joking either. My heart still aches when I think about that day—as much for her as for us.

Shortly after her showdown with the authorities, Ma did give us up for adoption, and Ellen and I never saw her again. To this day, I truly hope she is alive and well. I think about Ma and pray that, if she is alive, she has turned her life around. Maybe one day I'll try to find her. I've never had a strong desire to look for her—life-long anger, I guess. Still, I often find myself thinking about her.

The authorities had to look for Daddy to sign adoption papers. They eventually found him living in a town not too far away. He agreed to the adoptions. My Aunt Lynn told me he was hesitant about giving us up, but decided it would be best for Ellen and me. After our adoptions, Daddy started coming to see us in our new homes—Ellen and I had to be separated. Even though I was learning to accept my new home, my new parents and my new life, I wanted to understand what had happened to our family. I tried to discuss Ellen's and my adoption with Daddy, but each time he would change the subject. I finally realized how much it still pained him, so I stopped bringing it up. He continued visiting us—although we were good and grown— until about fifteen years ago when he remarried. I had a feeling his new wife had a lot to do with his second disappearance from our lives. He still kept in touch, but wouldn't see us. At least by then, Ellen and I were better able to handle his disappearance. We were much older.

One of the last times I saw him, though, he did say to me, "Your mother tried to get help several times, but couldn't stay away from the bottle for more than a couple of weeks." He said that he really didn't want to leave us, but felt that he had to go to maintain his own sanity. "Plus," he said, "Your mother hinted she would do something desperate if I tried to take you girls with me."

Cancer *of the* Spirit

Aunt Goldie and Uncle Rufus adopted Ellen. They already had two children. They also owned the neighborhood grocery store and had for many years. I was adopted by a well-to-do older couple, who'd always wanted children but weren't able to have any. We wanted to be together, but neither couple felt they could handle Ellen and me. Shortly after Ellen's adoption, Aunt Goldie and Uncle Rufus lost the store. A&G food chain opened in town and took away most of their business. Uncle Rufus went to work as a mechanic at a local gas station. Although Ellen's family was never as well off as mine, they always seemed much happier. There was always a lot of laughter in their home. I really envied that, but never let anyone know.

Both Ellen's and my adoptive parents were compassionate and considerate people. They allowed us to see each other as much as possible, and we were very grateful for that because we were so close. But we went to different schools and the circumstances of our separate adoptions caused our lives to unfold in extremely different ways.

For most of my life, I honestly believed I was the fortunate twin. In many ways, I was. But I have recently begun to question this. I'm currently facing a number of issues that have sparked a mind-boggling reassessment of my life without Daddy and Ma, and particularly, life with my adoptive parents, the Dechanels.

Mom and Dad Dechanel are considered role models. They've made numerous contributions to their community over the years and remain highly respected community members today, although Dad Dechanel had a drinking problem until about three years ago. But so do many of the men in his circle. During my childhood, and truthfully, until he stopped drinking, the unpleasant effects of his heavy drinking always brought back heart-aching memories of Ma.

Ife

Both Mom and Dad Dechanel, but especially Mom Dechanel, are to this day, die-hard middle-class folks—they take great pride in their fashionably furnished and tastefully decorated home, their sorority and fraternity memberships, and their church and community activities. Mom Dechanel is still an active member of Sigma Theta Alpha sorority and takes every opportunity, when she's feeling up to it, to host some classy purple and lilac affair.

My parents both retired long ago, but they're still dynamic and consistent churchgoers and have loyally attended their church and contributed to its prosperity, as well as to their community, for the last fifty-five years. They have chaired many church programs and worked extremely hard to ensure their success. Yet, even with the great sense of pride they have in their personal accomplishments, my adoption, as old as I am, still remains the highlight of their lives. Every opportunity they get, they travel to DC to visit with my family and me.

I was raised as an only child and was often told how pretty I was. I assumed it was because of how well mannered I was. However, I later learned it was because of my light-brown skin, dark features, and long black hair. This surprised me because when I was very young, I remembered Ma telling Ellen and me, "Pretty faces are a dime a dozen, and your actions speak louder than words." Mom Dechanel never told me that. She thought—and still thinks—that I am the most beautiful person on the face of the earth.

I was always the center of attention and the constant recipient of Mom and Dad Dechanel's and, for that matter, everyone else's love and affection. I was taught at an early age that there was nothing I couldn't accomplish, that nothing was beyond my reach. I was always impeccably groomed and dressed in the prettiest clothes. But even with all of the attention and encouragement I received, I never felt quite worthy or deserving of it. I often wondered what my life would have been like if I had not been given up for adoption.

I went to the very best schools in Winston-Salem. I learned to play the piano and had dance lessons. Mom and Dad Dechanel made sure I was involved in all the appropriate social activities for girls during every phase of my life. Everything was so wonderful. After graduating from high school, I was off to, where else, D.C. Teachers College, Mom Dechanel's alma mater. That's where I felt my life truly began. Although my primary goal was to get an education, Mom Dechanel advised me to "find a rich, handsome and intelligent man"—in that order, and her advice remained foremost in my mind. I loved D.C. from day one. My years at college were full of excitement, frivolous fun, and learning—not just academics but also learning the many lessons of life. By the time I left D.C. Teachers, memories of my birth mother had almost completely faded, at least I thought they had.

But, I didn't receive a degree from D.C. Teachers. I was just one semester short of graduating when I became pregnant and married Paul, my college sweetheart. Paul fit the bill perfectly in terms of Mom Dechanel's criteria. He was from a well-to-do family, handsome, and very intelligent. My marriage to Paul was short-lived though. Four months after the birth of our son, Malcolm, Paul died in a car accident. He and three of his frat brothers had gone to a fraternity party. I wanted him to stay at home with our new baby and me, but I knew that he really wanted to go. He hadn't hung out with his buddies since Malcolm was born. None of his friends had a car, so Paul was driving. I still regret that he was the one with the car. They were on their way home from that party. All of them had been drinking. Paul's surviving frat brother, Theron, said that Paul was speeding the wrong way up a one-way street when he crashed head-on into a truck. Remarkably, the truck driver wasn't injured, but Paul and his other two fraternity brothers were killed. Several of our friends who were at the party told me that Paul seemed so happy to be out and that he drank much more than he usually did. He probably felt a sense of freedom, something that he had probably missed since Malcolm's birth.

Whenever I'm around anyone who drinks too much—no offense to anyone here—I think about how my family was torn apart and never reunited because of alcohol. I have such a low tolerance for people who have a "few too many." Sometimes I still feel some guilt about the accident. I had asked—actually I had insisted—that Paul not go out with "the boys" once Malcolm was born. And then he overdid it when he finally did.

Paul's death left me deeply depressed for months. The love of my life was gone. My dream of living the "good life"—as part of a happy family with someone that I loved and who loved me—was shattered. Yet I remember thinking that although the accident ended Paul's life, it wouldn't end my relationship with him. I loved him and knew that part of me always would. And every time I look at Malcolm, it's like seeing Paul again. Malcolm's the breath of life that has brought me constant happiness.

But losing Paul triggered some of the same feelings of disappointment, fear, and loss that I felt when Daddy left, and when Ma and Daddy gave Ellen and me up for adoption. This happened again recently when Ellen died.

It took me about a year and a half to accept Paul's death. Around that time, one of my best friends invited me to a party. I accepted her invitation but was leery about going. Any mention of a party brought back painful memories of Paul's death. But I was really surprised at how much I enjoyed myself. Before it ended, I was happy I had decided to go because I met Leon. He was this bright, stunningly muscular, and seemingly gentle man. I couldn't believe it, but I was immediately attracted to him, as he was to me. It was a hot July day and I couldn't help but notice he was wearing a pair of tight fitting shorts. He looked 'reeeaaal' good! I particularly liked his perfectly sized solid butt. Butts are still my thing to this day. Although I had a good time at the party, I felt a strong sense of guilt. Right before the blue light was replaced with a regular 100-watt bulb, Leon asked me to go out with him. I told him I would let him know later. Three weeks later we had our first date, and so the romance began.

I spent a year and a half getting to know Leon, checking him out and observing the way he related to Malcolm. I was impressed with everything about him, and he truly adored me. After a two-year courtship, we were married. Leon was almost everything I had hoped for. He was not as well-to-do as I would have liked; but we both had good jobs, and our combined income allowed us to blend in well with the "bourgie" DC crowd. He had all of the qualities that really mattered—he was kind, loving, supportive, and honest, and just as important, he was committed, dedicated and devoted to me, and to Malcolm. He was also very devoted to his mom, who had raised her only child as a single mom.

Our first eight years were romance novel material. We really had it going on. During our ninth year, we had a beautiful baby girl—Alexis. Her birth was a bit of a surprise since we had been trying to have a baby for years. It took a week of uninterrupted romantic evenings spent at our favorite downtown hotel before Alexis was conceived. And from the beginning she has been an absolute delight to us and to Malcolm.

Ife

Our problems began three years after Alexis was born. Although Leon was a casual marijuana user from the time I met him, he had never shown any signs of having a drug problem. His casual use became more frequent. About five years ago my concern turned to worry when, contrary to his nature, Leon became short-tempered, impatient, and moody. As his old personality began to vanish, I began to suspect that he might be using other drugs. I talked to him about it, but he became angry and denied using anything other than marijuana. I still had my doubts, but I wanted to believe and trust him, so I did. To my knowledge, he had never lied to me before.

Several months later, I noticed a marked difference in the way he handled our finances. He had always taken such pride in his money management skills and our stellar credit rating. During the same period Leon began to mismanage our finances, he also spent less and less time at home in the evenings and began to disappear for days at a time. On nights that Leon didn't come home, he'd tell me that he had dropped by his mother's house and had fallen asleep. Of course, she always confirmed his story. She seemed to have no clue about what was happening to Leon. That's her baby boy, no matter how old he is.

But his disappearances let me know that my suspicions were not only right, but that his drug dependence was much worse than I had ever imagined. I also wondered if there was another woman. Leon had never given me any reason to suspect that, but you never know, especially given his condition. Our financial stability as well as our personal relationship began to fall apart. I began to worry that Leon was behaving the way he was because he was getting ready to leave me. I just didn't know. What I did know was that I couldn't handle another loss. I'd had more than my share of painful losses and felt I absolutely could not survive another. No way.

Cancer *of the* Spirit

I approached Leon again with my concerns and my suspicion that he was using stronger drugs than marijuana. Again, he denied using anything other than "weed." Then he verbally attacked me for making such an accusation. We argued then as we never had before, creating an atmosphere that seemed to penetrate the very walls of our home, a gloom so profound that it took me back to 1953 and our house on the day Daddy left us. To my astonishment and dismay, that day seemed so clear, so vivid, that the feeling it invoked frightened me. In a flash, the whole haunting issue of abandonment—an issue my heart had been harboring for years—erupted like lava from a reawakened volcano. That realization stunned me to silence. From that moment, I knew I would have to deal with that issue, and the fact that it had had me living in a state of denial for so long.

My abrupt silence allowed Leon to calm down, too. He began talking, trying to explain the pressure he felt from the frequent annoying phone calls from bill collectors. He even attempted to rationalize his increasingly frequent and lengthy absences from home. He eventually returned to the issue of drugs and although he admitted having tried a couple of other drugs, insisted that he wasn't using them on a regular basis. Of course, he was lying. But when I realized he knew that I knew he was lying, and he continued with that stupid lie, I was so outraged and hurt that I momentarily lost control and slapped the daylights out of him. He was stunned. Frankly, so was I. Never in my entire life had I ever before done anything like that. Leon's eyes told me that he wanted to hit me back, but he only said , "What the hell is wrong with you, woman?" slammed the door and left the house. I remember that scene as if it happened just yesterday.

I began to feel as though I were drowning in a deep pool of personal pain. And there was no one to save me—except Malcolm. Poor

Ife

Malcolm, even as a youngster, had been aware of my grief. He was so protective of me. Until recently, no one else knew my agony. I am quite good at faking appearances. Mom Dechanel taught me that. When she'd uncovered another of Dad Dechanel's many indiscretions, she'd say, "Things could be worse, honey," and continued as if nothing had happened. I guess that's what women "back in the day" were pro-grammed to do. So very much of their life was a masquerade, a facade, a lie—as is so much of mine. It all makes me feel so empty and sad.

And then there's Alexis, who's fourteen. I've always heard that the early teen years are when mothers and daughters begin bumping heads. The tension of puberty and all the other challenges of being a teenager, including peer pressure, just make things so difficult. But I never dreamed it would happen to Alexis and me. Until recently, we could discuss almost anything. We were so comfortable with each other. But that relationship seems to have evaporated. She's begun hanging out with a group of girls who, from my perspective, are headed down the road to destruction. They've already had a couple of run-ins with the law for suspected shoplifting and under-age drinking. Alexis was always such a sensible child, quite mature for her age. I suspect, though, that her behavior is a way of acting out her confusion and fear of her father's self-destructive behavior. He was her idol, and could do no wrong in her eyes. But now he's so consumed by his addiction that he can't help himself, let alone anyone else, not even Alexis, his pride and joy. She may even blame me for his behavior somehow, just as I blamed my mother for Daddy leaving. Justified or not, this is the way children sometimes think. Whenever I try to talk to her, she sucks her teeth and says, "Mom, I'm fine. You worry too much."

In spite of what she says, her grades have dropped to an all time low. This time last year she was an honor student, well on her way to receiving academic scholarships for college. Last week, during a parent-teacher conference, her English teacher asked me whether Alexis was having problems at home. I lied. I told her there was nothing out of the ordinary happening in my home. Telling that lie made me feel awful, but I was just too embarrassed to tell the truth. The shadow of Mom Dechanel is ever so present.

Malcolm, on the other hand, is now twenty-five and has been an absolute blessing in helping me with his little sister. He has adored her from the day she was born. Even with the eleven-year difference in their ages, there's always been a special bond between them. Alexis is much more willing to listen to and accept advice from Malcolm. When I watch the two of them together, I know we will somehow get through this, and emerge a little stronger individually and as a family. I just wish Leon were himself. We really need him now. We miss him so much, especially me.

Our problems and challenges seemed to be mounting so rapidly it was hard for me to cope. I felt as though I was losing control, with deep-seated feelings of abandonment, my husband's drug addiction, and my daughter's adolescent rebellion in the midst of it all. I felt mentally, physically, and spiritually exhausted. I found it difficult to sleep or concentrate and had practically no appetite, whereas food had always been a major source of enjoyment for me. I reached a point where I didn't even look like myself. The stress really had a frightening impact on me, its effects so invasive I felt I was no longer in touch with myself. It was as though so much of the real me had been lost over the years. Lost as a small abandoned child, lost as a young widow and lost as a virtually single parent.

Ife

From early on, I had learned to overcome whatever obstacles were placed in my path. Consequently, I was confident that I could and would take charge of, and eventually change my stressful, lonely and heartbreaking existence. Recently, I made the decision to search for the reasons for feeling lonely, unhappy, and, at times, bitter.

Although Mom Dechanel taught me that it is inappropriate to talk with friends about personal adversities, I've begun to confide in two very close and dear friends, Delbie and Lorna, something I would have never done in the past. To be truthful they're the only two friends who want to be around me these days. They've always confided in me and sought my advice about situations that have troubled them. That had always made me feel special despite that fact that sometimes I have felt a bit overwhelmed and pressured by their dependence. Over the years, though, Delbie and Lorna, in particular, have told me what a relief it has been to have someone to talk to and how much our "girl talk" helped them get through many hard times. Now that I have gathered enough nerve and heart to honestly share my feelings, I understand what they were saying. The idea of having them not only listen to my troubles, but also empathize with my feelings helps me deal with my concerns.

The first time I confided in them, the three of us had gone to dinner at our favorite restaurant, Visions of the Sea, near Union Station. We talked for hours, late into the evening. I did most of the talking. Sometimes it was hard for me to get through what I was saying. They were astonished at my confessions, especially about Leon. It was reflected in their eyes—and all over their faces. Both Delbie and Lorna had had such high regard and admiration for Leon; they just didn't want to believe he was not the man they thought they had come to know. As close as I am to the situation, it's even hard for me to believe some-times. Lorna admitted that she suspected something was wrong, but had no idea what it was. I was relieved when they both shared my conclusion that Leon was not having an affair. I felt so grateful that night—having two sincere friends to really listen to me and care about me at that most vulnerable time. It was a true blessing. Our tears left many wet spots on the beautiful tablecloth that night. I know the waitress wondered what was going on. Since that night, at least one of them calls me daily to see how I'm doing.

Have you ever had the feeling that a weight has been lifted from your mind, body, and soul? That's exactly how I felt after that night. Although this is only one of many steps to my becoming whole again, sharing my deepest concerns and feelings with my two most trusted friends is a major breakthrough for me. It's helped me face, head-on, one of the most troubling issues in my life—the sense that my whole life has been a masquerade, a lie I've lived by not being who I really am and who I really want to be. Until now, I never realized how inhibiting and hurtful this has been. But finally, the hard work of rediscovering my true self, and my recovery, have truly begun.

Another action I have taken and, I must tell you, most reluctantly, is to seek professional guidance to help me face the many issues I am currently dealing with. Dr. Harlee, a therapist recommended by Lorna, is patient, kind, and sensitive. She has allowed me to move slowly through a process that I had no idea would take so long. I'm really amazed, and pleased, at how introspective I'm becoming. At times the process has been very painful—shaming and heartbreaking. At other times it's enlightening, heart-warming, and joyous. My once-a-week sessions have generated a lot of tears and heartache, and some laughter as well. Sometimes it takes something drastic to introduce you to your own pain, and seeing a therapist is certainly drastic for me. The revelations I've experienced during the sessions have given me positive insight on, first, how to successfully cope with my own day-to-day challenges, and second, how best to encourage Leon to seek the professional help he needs to resolve many of the hidden and painful issues I now realize he's facing.

While delving into my childhood abandonment issue, I began to understand my continuing fear that Leon would pick up and leave me one day. Dr. Harlee helped me see that I have unconsciously communicated this feeling to Leon for the last twenty-three years and that it now has been partially realized through his disappearing for days at a time. Dr. Harlee also let me know that while I cannot blame myself for Leon's destructive behavior, I may be contributing to it. She also made me understand that when it's all said and done, Leon is an adult and is responsible for his own actions and their consequences—not me.

Still, I've learned that the way I've handled many situations over the years could be directly related to my subconsciously seeking an outcome I so fear. After all, Daddy did leave me and Ma put me up for adoption. Why would anyone else want me? My very own self-fulfilling prophesy. Heavy stuff, isn't it? In my mind, Mom and Dad Dechanel were the only exceptions.

Dr. Harlee has helped me to really begin to love myself by helping me focus on my strong points. However, I must admit that one of my remaining weak points is that I'm still a little bitter about Daddy leaving, and Ma giving Ellen and me up for adoption; these two events so influenced my life. They made me insecure and fearful. But I'm committed to working hard to let this go. Dr. Harlee has also helped me understand and accept that I am a responsible, devoted, loving, and caring wife, mother, and friend. And I can now accept the fact that life throws all of us a few curve balls just to help prepare us for the unexpected and difficult times. A most important insight that I had during one of my sessions was that Daddy leaving, and me being put up for adoption, have nothing to do with my worth as a human being, but rather something to do with Daddy's and Ma's own insecurities and problems. Before these sessions, I wouldn't have considered that they were suffering from their own feelings of inadequacy. Years ago, Daddy hinted at some challenges of his own. I may never know what feelings of inadequacy made him do what he did, but at least I now understand that possibility. Another thing I now know is that having been abandoned by both my parents will, to some degree, be a life-long issue for me. But at least I'm consciously working to eradicate some of the adverse effects. Now that I have already had some success in doing that has certainly nourished my once nearly depleted soul.

Another thing I now completely understand is that priorities change as conditions change. This concept was completely foreign to me before my sessions with Dr. Harlee. Re-establishing the positive, loving, and trusting relationship Alexis and I once shared is now my primary priority. Through my in-depth conversations with Dr. Harlee, I have created, in theory at least, ways that may get us back to where we were before Leon's problems consumed us all and before the peer pressure set in.

Dr. Harlee has been a tremendous help to me. My damaged spirit is becoming healthier with each session. Not only do I have a real sense of empowerment, I think I can now also accept it—something I don't think I could have truthfully done in the past. I can also accept and understand that a healthy and positive self-image is my right, perhaps even my responsibility. To help me continue my forward advancement, Dr. Harlee suggested that I make a conscious effort to do at least one thing for myself everyday, no matter how small. And she urged me to set aside a jar in which to put a quarter every time I actually do something for myself; the goal is then to take that "reward money" after a year's time and buy myself something special. She said I will be astonished at how this action alone will make me conscious of acknowledging myself, not to mention how much I will have saved after a year. She suggested allowing myself ten or fifteen minutes a day to read a favorite novel or taking a relaxing bubble bath, "Just do something—anything," she said, "Something for your mind, body, and soul." I have relentlessly followed this advice, and all I can say is—what a great feeling!

The final and most difficult thing that I have done to reclaim the essence of who I am, is to always listen to my inner spirit and make decisions based on my overall well-being. I have learned that this is something most of us women find very difficult to do. We are usually the primary care givers, the nurturers and the perceived pillars of strength for everyone. We tend to care for everyone before we care for ourselves. This is, and always has been, a bad decision. If we don't take care of ourselves first—mentally, physically, and spiritually—what good can we really be to others? Besides, in most cases, we perpetuate their dependence on us, not them. Women must learn to look deep within themselves—their hearts, their souls, and their minds—and determine what it is that they really want, and more important, what they need, and then, what they have to do to achieve their goals.

I'm a little embarrassed for sharing all of this, but thanks for listening and supporting me.

Chapter Three

Dominique
Age: 37 - Iowa City, IA

I may not have known Kay as well as some of you. I do, though, understand the importance of the support of friends and loved ones when problems seem overwhelming.

Like Helen, part of my problem was my husband; but it seems our adversities have returned him to me as, once again, my best friend. At least that's what I'm hoping. It may surprise some of you to learn that my husband is Black. However you may feel about that, I hope you won't mind listening to what I have to say, too.

My "beginning" is much later than Helen's. It was 1979, and I was 17. I remember trying to ignore the old 1959 aqua and white Chevy that pulled up beside me as I walked down Main Street. Although the guy behind the wheel was really cute, I thought he had a lot of nerve hollering out of his window at a white girl. It was 1979 and in Iowa City, Iowa, a college town where interracial relationships were on the rise. But still, I immediately thought of the stories my parents had told me about Black men being lynched for being suspected of looking at a white woman, not to mention hollering at one. The driver kept on calling, "Hey pretty lady, want a ride?" which finally prompted me to say, "No thank you, not today."

I was born in the early sixties, and don't personally know much about the racism that divided Blacks and whites during that time and before. However I was certainly aware of the prejudices my parents had about Black people and "their habits." When Black people started moving into our cozy lily-white neighborhood in the mid-sixties, the entire neighborhood was horrified. My parents, being racists themselves, fed into the neighborhood's "going to pot" frenzy. Their attitudes about Blacks and other minorities began to change, however, when they continued to participate in the Neighborhood Civic Association after most of the white families moved out. For the first time, they had an opportunity to work closely with Blacks and other minorities. In so doing, they saw for themselves the foolishness of the frenzy. In fact, they have only seen improvements in their neighborhood, which is now a very integrated one in Iowa City. Forty years later, my parents are still living there.

By the time I was ten years old, my parents had become "reformed racists." Given their earlier convictions, and later through their own action, I think they did a damn good job of showing my brother and me what racial equality was really about.

From junior high school on, Black people fascinated me. The few in my classes always seemed so sure of themselves. Many of my classmates referred to them as "uppity niggers," but I admired the "hip" way they talked, the way some of the Black guys bopped when they walked, those luscious full lips, and hair that didn't have to be washed every day. I learned that while taking gym classes. The cultural differences

Cancer *of the* Spirit

intrigued me; they still do, even though I have been very close to it all for years now. I had secretly admired Black people long before that day on Main Street when I decided to be daring and to free the risk-taking side of me that had lain dormant for so long.

Although I tried to be coy, I was glad when the guy continued to drive slowly next to me as I walked. When we got near the pizza shop, he yelled out, "Want a slice of pizza and a soda?" To my own surprise, I said, "Why not?" After all, I was hungry. For ten solid months after that pepperoni pizza and coke, Jerome and I were inseparable. Black women couldn't stand it! They were very resentful, and didn't try to hide it either.

"They still don't", shouted Ena.

White men were worse; they could be kind of scary. But in spite of the nasty stares, frowns of disgust, and foul comments, we did everything together. We didn't care; we were in love. Before our eleventh month together, we decided to run away and get married.

Luckily, my parents had become extremely fond of Jerome, so they weren't too upset when we told them we were married. That's when I really knew my parents had overcome their prejudices. Their acceptance of the marriage of their only daughter to a Black man was the most profound proof of their transformation I could ask for! My brother also liked Jerome; he thought he was cool and was very happy for us. I'm sorry that I can't say the same of Jerome's parents. They weren't receptive of me before we got married, and were even less receptive immediately afterward. We had been married for several months before they slowly began warming up to me. They could easily see how much I loved their son. I also think that once they met my family and saw how genuinely unprejudiced we all were, they succumbed.

Ife

Today, they treat me like a daughter. And it doesn't hurt that I'm the mother of two of their grandchildren. What a difference that has made.

I was almost eighteen and Jerome was nineteen when we got married. We had been married for several months when it struck me that we had stopped going to parties and other social functions where mostly Black people would be attending, unless it was a family activity. We attended some parties where mostly white people would be, but not that many. I asked Jerome what was going on; I wanted to know if he was ashamed of having a white wife. He told me, although without much conviction, that I was being foolish. Hurt and angry, I reminded him that he didn't seem too ashamed of having a white girlfriend. I truly resented him not taking me out anymore, because before we were married, we accepted any—and everybody's invitation, and went everywhere together. We always had a ball. But I was young and in love and couldn't stand to have any anger come between us. So, with some reservation, I decided not to hassle him about it.

After Jerome and I had been married for three years, we agreed to have a baby. I stopped taking birth control pills and just knew I would get pregnant right away. Three years later, nothing had happened. I think we had been trying too hard. At least that is what our doctor told us. He suggested several techniques that would help us unwind a little before our playtime. Three months after that, I became pregnant. We were both very happy, and our parents were thrilled. On June 4, 1986, we had a 7 pound, 8 ounce baby girl and named her Rebecca. She had big blue eyes like mine, and her father's beautiful dark brown skin and nose. She was a pleasant child from day one. As an infant, she never cried unless she was hungry or wet. Her little sister Amy, on the other hand, born two years later, cried constantly. The poor child had colic.

Cancer *of the* Spirit

Still, Rebecca loved her dearly and would often try to comfort her by rubbing her tummy when she cried.

Growing up, Rebecca was kind of tom-boyish. From the age of two and a half, she loved competitive games, including sports. She competed with little boys as vigorously as she did with little girls and usually won—especially playing basketball and soccer. She always had such a winning attitude. By the time she was eight, she was a real little athlete. Sometimes she was so rough, I feared she would get hurt. And until three years ago, she never did. She was in her last year at Kramer Junior High School. I never will forget that phone call from her track coach.

It was on a Monday. The phone rang shortly after I got home from work. It was Coach Aldridge. She said Rebecca had taken a fall during a practice run for the track meet the next Saturday, and she wasn't certain, but thought that Rebecca had broken her left leg. Panic stricken, I rushed out of the house, with Amy right behind me. She'd heard my conversation with Coach Aldridge and was just as panicked as I was. She and Rebecca were, and still are, so close. When we arrived at the school, an ambulance was already there. Amy and I rode to Memorial Hospital in the ambulance with Rebecca. As usual, she was in good spirits and told us not to worry. She was so upbeat that you would have never known how much pain she was in. Instead of Amy and me cheering her up, she was cheering us up. That was unbelievable.

On the way to the hospital, I realized I had not contacted Jerome; so when we got there, Amy stayed with Rebecca while I called him. He was there in no time flat. By that time, I had completed all of the necessary paperwork and Rebecca's x-rays were finished. They confirmed that she had, not one, but two bad breaks. That news upset all of us, except Rebecca. She told us, "You've got to take life as it comes, and deal with it in a positive way. I'll be fine, I promise you. I'll miss running, but I'll get back to it."

Rebecca was fine for the first four days after the cast was put on her leg.   On the morning of the fifth day after her accident—the very Saturday of the track meet—she began to complain about not feeling so well. I knew something was wrong because Rebecca never complained. When she didn't improve and continued to feel bad all that morning and into the early afternoon, we took her to the emergency room in the late afternoon. As we waited, Amy sat by Rebecca's side, rubbing her head and holding her hand.

Within ten minutes of our arrival a strange look came over Rebecca's face. She turned to me and said, "I really don't feel well," and before she could say anything more, suddenly, violently her body began to convulse and Rebecca lost consciousness. Amy began to cry uncontrollably. Jerome's entire body began to shake as he held her. The doctors and nurses immediately began to attend to Rebecca, trying to resuscitate her, but she didn't respond. Rebecca had slipped into a coma. The doctors had no idea why. We were swiftly escorted from the emergency room. I didn't want to leave Rebecca's side, but I knew there was nothing I could do for her. Meanwhile both Amy and Jerome were distraught. It took all I had to comfort them when I desperately needed comforting myself. I felt helpless, my heart ached, my spirit was torn, and I was so afraid. For the next four days, my family practically lived at Memorial Hospital. Jerome did go home to get us fresh clothes and toiletries, but, despite the agonizing stress, we simply couldn't leave.

Cancer *of the* Spirit

On the third day after Rebecca went into her coma, the doctors determined that she'd had a severe allergic reaction to one of the medications she'd been given. She didn't seem to be getting any better, but rather going deeper and deeper into the coma. The medical staff became very concerned because allergic reactions could sometimes be fatal. When they told me that, a painful cramp knotted my stomach. It was indescribable. Those words and that pain still resonate in me today.

Regardless of what those doctors said, I refused to believe my daughter was going to die. Because we needed to believe that she could hear us, Jerome, Amy, and I talked to Rebecca constantly. For the next four days we read poetry, sang her favorite songs, passed on news about her best friends, and recited her favorite passages from the Bible. Many of her friends and teachers from Kramer came by to see her. Still, at times, Jerome and Amy were almost hysterical. I tried my best to comfort them while I concealed my gut-wrenching pain and heart-breaking sorrow.

On the fifth day of Rebecca's coma, the nurses and doctors insisted that we go home and try and get some rest. We had been at the hospital around the clock for four days. Needless to say, we were all exhausted. Since there really was nothing we could do for Rebecca, we decided to take their advice and went home. That trip home was one of many more to come.

Rebecca lay in a coma for nearly a year. Our minister faithfully visited every Saturday and prayed with us for Rebecca's recovery. Even though I never gave up hope, the eleven and a half months that Rebecca was "somewhere else" were the toughest and loneliest days of my life. I encouraged Jerome and Amy to go on with their lives and did my best to assure them I would too; but the pretense caught up with me. My boss suggested that I take a leave-of-absence because my job as an accounting technician required focused attention, which I could no longer give. All my thoughts were with Rebecca. My life became consumed with her, so much so that I had unconsciously stopped paying any attention to Jerome and Amy.

This was undoubtedly an excuse for Jerome seeking comfort elsewhere, but this was not the first time he had been unfaithful. As in the past, I learned of Jerome's infidelity purely by accident. This time, it was through a nurse who was on duty one evening during our visit with Rebecca. When Jerome walked into the room ahead of Amy and me, I heard the nurse say, "Hi, I know you. You're Paula's guy, aren't you?" His reaction and the look on his face told me the rest of the story. When the nurse saw me and realized I was his wife, she knew she had "put her foot in her mouth," but didn't appear to be the least bit sorry. However, she did apologize and quickly left the room.

Jerome tried to give some inane explanation, but I shoved him aside and told him to shut up and cut the bullshit. I couldn't stand to hear another word from his sorry ass. Excuse my language, but I still get upset and angry when I talk about it. Just looking at Jerome made me sick. Rebecca was lying there possibly dying; Amy standing there frozen in a state of fear and shock at witnessing such an unpleasant exchange between her dad and me—especially, under the circumstances. I sensed that Amy was scared to death of what might happen to our family. That was more than enough for me to handle at that moment. As he had in the past, he begged my forgiveness, and, again, promised it would never happen again. But this time I was angry. I asked myself, "How could he, in the middle of this crisis, be so callous?"

Cancer *of the* Spirit

Still, I really didn't have the energy to deal with him then. Every ounce of me was devoted to Rebecca's recovery.

Unable to control themselves, several of the women couldn't help but comment: "What a low-down dirty dog." "How dare he!" "That scumbag!"

After that incident, Amy and I spent as much time as we could with Rebecca, praying for her recovery. Her doctors said that even if she did regain consciousness, she would more than likely suffer some degree of brain damage. But, again, I refused to accept their prognosis. I immediately blocked it out of my mind. I had become good at that—blocking things, I mean.

Late one night in August, we got a call from the hospital telling us to get there as quickly as we could. There had been a change in Rebecca's condition. The doctor said they didn't expect her to make it through the night. I screamed, "Oh, my God!" and immediately dropped to my knees and prayed to God to spare my baby's life. The thought of losing my child was more agonizing than I could bear. When we got to the hospital, Rebecca's breathing was labored. She was fighting for her life and I couldn't contain my grief. I completely "lost it." Thank God Amy was there. I had never realized how strong she was until then. She was such a great comfort to me that night. Jerome stayed at Rebecca's bedside reciting poetry that he had often read to her when she was younger. A nurse was also there, watching Rebecca's every move and a doctor was never far away. Suddenly Rebecca began coughing—a choking, hacking cough. The nurse and a doctor rushed to her, holding her to keep her from dislodging her feeding tube or hurting herself on the monitors. Jerome, Amy and I began to panic. Her coughing fit seemed to last forever. Then, miraculously—because I know it was nothing less than a miracle—Rebecca opened her eyes. We were all too astonished to speak. Rebecca, naturally, was confused, disoriented, and still quite groggy. She looked around as if she was silently asking, "What happened?" That was the most incredible moment of my life. Jerome, Amy and I—and even the doctor and nurse—began laughing and crying, both at the same time. Within two hours of waking up, Rebecca was able to talk and answer questions, but she didn't recognize any of us. It was obvious she was nowhere near functioning to full mental or physical capacity; and the doctors still had to thoroughly examine and observe her before they could make any predictions about brain damage. I quite honestly was afraid to be too happy about Rebecca. I was of course ecstatic about her regaining consciousness, but the fact that she didn't know who I was broke my heart, and I realized the possibility that she might not ever remember me.

Two agonizing weeks after Rebecca's reawakening, I arrived at the hospital earlier than usual one morning. When I entered her room, Rebecca smiled at me. Although it was faint, it was the same smile she had always given me when she was glad to see me. I knew she recognized me. I think my legs gave out because I found myself kneeling beside her bed thanking God and crying for joy.

Rebecca remained in the hospital another month after that and made remarkable progress. Her doctors were truly amazed. They, too, called her recovery a miracle. By the time she was released, her mental capacities were almost back to normal. Her physical capacities were still quite impaired and she had to undergo intense physical therapy for months, but she had come back to us. We brought her home to complete her recovery. A physical therapist visited her three times a week.

Cancer *of the* Spirit

Through it all, Rebecca was anxious to get back to school and swore that she would run track again; and I'm overjoyed to say that I believe she will.

Jerome and I had been so consumed by what was happening with Rebecca, we had put our own troubles on a back burner. But given Rebecca's remarkable progress, I decided it was time for Jerome and me to have a heart-to-heart talk. I confronted him and asked him to be honest with me. I asked if he wanted a divorce and whether his answer would have any relevance to the fact that I'm white. I also wanted to know just how he felt the color of my skin had affected his life. It became apparent that my being white had had a more profound effect on him than I'd realized. His reaction to my questions indicated clearly that his answers would be coming from his heart.

He confessed that, over the years, he had felt very uneasy about us socializing with his Black friends because they always hassled him about me. He admitted that before we got married, those same friends were envious of him. It was fashionable back then, having a white girlfriend. Black guys loved it. He told me marriage, however, changed all that, and that he was surprised when he couldn't handle the hassling and, at the same time, felt like a coward for letting it dictate his behavior toward me. The way Rebecca and Amy were sometimes treated as children of a mixed marriage was also a source of pain for him. They have been badgered, even beaten once, and often ostracized in our community and at school. He almost broke down when he talked about how that had torn him apart. To escape his feelings of inadequacy as a husband and father, he began having affairs to make himself feel more like a man, and usually chose Black women because that seemed to lessen the conflict that raged within him.

Ife

Despite his honesty I was angry. I told him, as far as I was concerned, there never had been, and never would be, any excuse for betraying someone who you love, particularly someone who loves and trusts you completely. I also let him know he was not the only one to suffer at the hands of "friends" because of racism, that the reason my girlfriends Peggy and Alice stopped hanging out with me was because I married him. They'd all pretended to be so happy when we got married, but within a very short time, I knew that they weren't. One by one they began breaking dates, making excuses for why they couldn't hang out anymore; one by one they removed themselves from my life. I reminded him that even he had asked several times what had happened to them. I admitted that I always gave him some reason other than the real one. I also let him know that for a long time the loneliness was very difficult for me to take. Jerome didn't seem surprised by my revelations, but I could tell he was a little hurt mainly for me.

Jerome and I also discussed something he already knew. Other than my immediate family—my mother, father, and brother—my family has disassociated themselves from us. Before we got married, I never realized how deeply racism had affected their minds and hearts. Initially I was very hurt, but now I just feel sorry for their pathetic souls. For quite some time, Jerome ignored their stupidity, yet felt guilty about the situation because he knew how it hurt me.

What has bothered both Jerome and me more than anything else, is the way our children have been treated because they are from an interracial marriage. I've always felt that our answers to many of the questions about racism that Rebecca and Amy asked were insufficient. Still despite our inability to address their concerns, despite my extended family's disassociation, despite public ostracism, the badgering and beatings, our daughters have done remarkably well in handling these situations. To experience what they have, I can emphatically say how proud Jerome and I are to be the parents of two children with such positive, healthy attitudes, and glowing spirits.

During our talk, for the first time, I was honest with Jerome about many of the difficulties I had encountered as a result of being married to him. I wanted him to know that he was not alone in dealing with ambivalent feelings about marrying someone of a different race. It's too bad we had never talked about our feelings before. Our life together might well have been very different, and probably much more positive.

Jerome is really trying to clean up his act. We are "dating" again— hanging out at some of the nicer places in town—and really talking and listening to one another. Over the last couple of months, he has even gone to church with the girls and me a few times. I can see some positive change in him.

We know it's inevitable that we will continue to face trials for choosing to marry outside of our race, but I believe we are finally ready to tackle those trials straight up— together as a family. And I am a much stronger, wiser, confident individual, and know I can overcome any adversity that comes my way. Having come through Rebecca's extraordinary ordeal, I believe I can conquer anything now.

Ife

Chapter Four

Ena
Age: 23 - Charlotte, NC

In case any of you didn't quite hear my comment when Dominique was sharing her story, I admit to being one of those Black women who don't like to see white women taking our men. There are, as far as I'm concerned, too few good ones to share. After hearing what she had to say, though, I can better understand how circumstances can be similar to all women. If it's all right with everyone, I'd like to share experiences similar to Dominique's that I'm facing in dealing with the love of my life.

I'm Ena, for those of you who may not remember my name. Like Helen, I'm from North Carolina—Charlotte. Before I heard Miss Helen's and Miss Dominique's stories, I thought my problems were monumental. I should have known better since I'm the youngest one here—I think. Instead of just trying to tell you what's up with me, I've decided to read from my journal. I carry it with me everywhere, but this will be my first time sharing it with anyone. For some reason I really feel safe here.

Cancer *of the* Spirit

Let me first say that during my trip here, I spent time reviewing what I've confided in these pages. I knew many of the entries would be depressing. You see, I had already begun to question my on-again, off-again relationship with Ali, my boyfriend. I figured, with the new year fast approaching, now would be the perfect time to do a little soul-searching. I figured that reading my journal, reliving the ups and downs of the past year and a half with Ali, would help me realistically weigh the pros and cons of our relationship, but somehow, it seemed to only confuse me more.

Before I begin, let me give you a little background info. My boyfriend, Ali, is Jamaican. His family is fairly well to do so they could afford to send him to the United States for his schooling. His parents are divorced and live in Jamaica but they visit regularly, but separately. His father's very nice; his mother is barely cordial, but we get along. He's got a younger sister, Crystal; she's a nice kid, but you'll hear more about her later. Ali's been here for eight years now and plans to stay. I met him a year and a half ago at the Gateway, this classy Caribbean restaurant and club in Charlotte. Three of my girlfriends and I were celebrating my twenty-first birthday. We were getting our groove on when I noticed some brothers checking us out. We couldn't stay off the dance floor that night—the music was live. When we finally sat down, Ali and two of his boys came over to our table. None of us were impressed with any of them and wished they would move on. His boys got the message and left, but Ali didn't. He asked me to dance. I really didn't feel like it, but with some coaxing from my girls, I did. I intentionally danced badly. I figured that would get rid of him. It didn't—probably because he had already checked me out. One thing became quite apparent—Ali truly knows how to party, and I did like that about him.

Ife

After a couple more dances, Ali said he would like to see me again and asked for my phone number. I didn't want to give it to him, but my girlfriends said he was kinda cute, plus they were really impressed with his dancing. They said since I wasn't seriously dating anyone, giving Ali my number couldn't hurt anything. I'd always liked having at least two boyfriends at a time, and I did at the time, but my girls convinced me to give him a chance. Besides, I figured he wouldn't call anyway; and I was almost right. He finally called after three weeks. That's how we started, so I guess it's as good a place as any to begin.

July 17, 2001: *About 10 o'clock tonight the phone rings. I'm thinking it's Brina calling to tell me about her hot date with that cop she met while speeding. Instead, it was Ali, that guy I met at the Gateway. His voice sounded so different on the phone, almost sexy. I was surprised, I must admit, but somewhat glad to hear from him. He said he's been very busy the last couple of weeks, moving from one apartment to another one and getting set up. Wanted me to know he wasn't trying to play me.*

We talked for over an hour. I learned a lot about him, just as he did about me. Turns out his younger sister, Crystal, is coming from Jamaica to go to school and will be staying with him. That's why he had to get a bigger place. Until she arrives, he's the only member of his family living here. Although he didn't seem very excited about her coming, he's behaving very responsibly about it, knowing he's expected to look out for her. Seems since he was about six years old, his parents have been making him a responsible young man, giving him daily and weekly chores that were his responsibility alone. If he didn't do them, his privileges were immediately taken away; if he did, he was well rewarded. So from early on, he learned to be reliable and serious and learned about the rewards that go hand-in-hand with doing what you're counted on to do. My kind of upbringing!!

Not only that, he has a Bachelor of Science degree but doesn't seem to be doing much with it. His main interest is soccer; he's a star player on his team. They've even won a couple of championships. He's real proud of that. He says his nine-to-five pays his bills and that's good enough for now; says he doesn't have to "represent" yet, which I kinda understand, seeing as where I'm still living at home myself (though not for much longer—YES—since I got approved for that apartment near campus). Ali seemed surprised, but pleased, to know I'm working on my Masters in anthropology—claims he doesn't know too many "party girls" with brains and beauty, too. I don't know where he's been, cause Charlotte is full of us—maybe too full.

"I know that's right," yells Makeba.

August 24, 2001: *Mom and Dad warned me that moving into my own place would give me a taste of what it's like in the real world. Well, I sure the hell know what they meant. Since moving here, paying my rent and bills, working and going to school, I am busted, broke, and exhausted. But with all that, I am not sorry. I'm loving the freedom to be me. And the freedom to be with Ali, especially now that we've "become an item," as they used to say. It's hard for me to believe I feel this way after going out with him only, what, five or six times. But I have to admit he is just so outgoing and fun loving; he's got a really exciting personality, not to mention that Jamaican persistence. Everywhere we go, he's usually the center of attention, and he thrives on it. If I didn't think so highly of myself, I might be pressed. Thank goodness, my self-esteem is intact.*

Another plus is Crystal. She is smart and confident and seems to have a good affect on Ali. He's changed his attitude about work quite

Ife

a bit since Crystal arrived. Soccer is still a major part of his life, but he's taking his nine-to-five much more seriously, even got a promotion! I really think we're both on track to becoming mature adults!"

Although I know reading these pages is reading about my life, it's hard to believe that a person's life can go through so many changes, so many levels of social evolution, within the span of only a few months. When I look back at my life and all that has gone on before and think about all that is yet to come, I am amazed at how much the heart can endure. More than half of these pages bring back such warm, delightful memories—memories of fun-filled days and nights, of new adventures, romantic trips, and much more. Yet they lie against entries unfolding more pain and heartache than I thought was possible. The next entry I'll read is dated September 21, 2001.

"I still can't believe I'm playing hooky from school this week! Today is our third day in St. Maarten—a fantastic retreat. This is the first time that either of us has been to this glorious paradise. Although Ali is biased toward Jamaica, he loves this place as much as I do. This is my first trip to anywhere outside the United States. The only place I can compare it to is Hilton Head; and that doesn't even come close. I can't imagine how too many other places could be as beautiful as it is here. It's so lush! Tomorrow we will do a little sightseeing, since we only have two more days here. So far we have spent our time enjoying each other. Ali is treating me like the queen that I am. I'm happily accommodating him as well. More than half of our days are spent in bed. We've had room service almost every evening. When we do go out, we find the most romantic spot that we can—and there are plenty of them. We even spent one evening on Dawn Beach. Getting away is fantastic! It has brought new meaning to the word romance. That's enough journaling for today. I'm getting back to the reason we're here."

Cancer *of the* Spirit

But then on January 14, 2002 - *"Today Brina told me that Ali musta been thinking he was a player or something, when he tried to make a move on her. She thought he was playing around at first, but when she saw he wasn't, she was shocked and pissed off! Brina is my girl! We go way back and know all of each other's business, so I know she'd never lie to me. I may have my doubts about a couple of my other "friends", but not Brina. She said she was so mad she jumped dead on his case; Brina told Ali that she was going to tell me what happened so I would know what a dog he is. She said he begged her not to say anything to me, told her he wouldn't try to hit on her again; but she wasn't going for that, and told me right away. After she saw how upset I was, she was sorry she told me but still thought I should know. She's right, of course; I certainly would have told Brina if the situation had been reversed. But that doesn't help the pain and this feeling of betrayal.*

When I approached Ali about this, he said without hesitation "my bad, my bad" and said he didn't know what he was thinking about. Bullshit! He said he would never do anything to intentionally hurt me, and that he was wrong. Trying to hit on Brina! Did he think that wouldn't hurt me? Or I guess he just figured she'd never tell. That's just low.

I guess I'll get over it—I hope. I'll just have to see. For now, though, I don't want to see him. I insisted that we stop seeing each other. I just can't stand to look at him right now.

Well, that lasted about a minute. I'm sure some of ya'll know about that. Things went back to being okay for us for a while. Until . . . oh, right, here it is: March 5, 2002, 6:05 pm: - *" I ran into Crystal at the mall today. We decided to get something to eat and ended up talking. Crystal unintentionally told me some stuff—that she thought I already knew—about one of Ali's ex-girlfriends back in Jamaica. Trying to be tricky, I asked her, "So, do you think Ali will ever get over, oh, what's her name? You know, that one from high school." I think I realized it was too much information as soon as Crystal said she didn't think Ali would ever completely get over Palar, especially since he thought Palar's baby was really his son. Seems Ali and Palar were inseparable during their last two years of school. Crystal said Palar always thought she was 'all that' and that Palar was known to be a fast thing; Ali's parents didn't care for her at all. So when Palar became pregnant in their last year, Ali's parents weren't too happy. They were relieved, though, when Palar told everyone that the baby was not Ali's. Of course, Ali wasn't too happy about it because he thought they loved each other. In fact, he was so hurt, he was out of it for a couple of months. Crystal said he still gets a little sad about the whole thing.*

I guess the expression on my face told Crystal that I hadn't known any of this; she seemed really pressed once she realized I didn't know about Palar, this undying love, or this baby. Ali and I talked about ex-loves, but he never mentioned Palar. Maybe he didn't tell me because the situation is still too painful for him to talk about—having your girl get pregnant by someone else is pretty rough on the male ego. But if the memories are still that painful almost nine years later, just what does that mean? This really sucks! What else has Ali not told me? This has really dampened my spirit. Knowing me, this will cause me to doubt other things he says, and that's not good. Well, I'll see what he says when I ask him about Palar tonight. I think it may be time for another retreat."

March 5, 2002 - (Midnight) - *"After talking with Ali about his relationship with Palar, I can see why he wouldn't trust any woman again. Once he got over his anger at Crystal for telling me about her, he real-*

Cancer *of the* Spirit

ly opened up to me about Palar. She dogged him big time. Ali was really quite naive back then and trusted her to a fault, as he later found out. As he talked I thought, "Dag, that could have been me, the way I used to like having several guys to date all at the same time." Palar clearly got around a lot more than Ali knew, and had her own agenda. Ultimately, that agenda did not include him. She is now married to her baby's daddy—at least the one she claims to be the daddy—a rich older man, who gives her all of the material things she wants. When Ali found out what a liar Palar is, it made him question whether or not the baby is his. From what he told me, I think he still misses her, in some strange and crazy way. Oh well."

My May 11, 2002, entry is an extremely personal one. I'm debating whether or not to share it with you. I even dreaded having to write it. Well, I'm going to go on and share it. This entry reads: *"I ran into Raheem today. This is too wack to be true, but then . . .. I don't know how to begin, so I'll just say Raheem suggested that Ali and two of his boys may be on the down low. This is tearing me apart!!! Rah has been a good friend since fifth grade. He's always had my back, as I've had his. Rah said the word is out that Ali and his boys hang out at Popular, that gay club. That alone doesn't bother me so much, because a lot of straight people also hang out there. But Rah says people are talking about how Ali and these two guys always seem to be having a whole lot of fun when they're together. And it made me realize that I do have concerns about the amount of time Ali spends with his boys. I hadn't thought that much about it though, not until I saw Rah today.*

When I talked to Ali about how often he hangs out at Popular with his boys, he didn't confirm or deny it. He just laughed and said, "Ena, please! Give me a break!" I didn't feel comfortable with that response, but I also didn't feel comfortable taking that conversation to the next

47

Ife

level, so I let it go. But this is yet another mind blowing ordeal. I love Ali so much, but I can't deal with a man who is "dealing" with guys. I suppose it's possible that Ali and his boys could be more than just friends, but I really can't believe it in my heart. I certainly hope not!!"

November 1, 2002, 1 a.m. - *Lately, I've been focusing on my feelings and trying to make an honest assessment of where I'm coming from. I suppose that's why I keep reviewing my journal. These pages speak the truth about what I was feeling when they were written. Writing what I'm feeling helps me clarify my thoughts, clear away the BS so that all that's left is what's true for me. I read these pages and realize I have some important decisions to make.*

On the surface, Ali seems to be a wonderful person, and in so many ways he really is. Yet after reading through my journal—over and over again—I still have so many unanswered questions and doubts about our relationship. I'm not at all comfortable with what's going on. I've always dreamed of a relationship in which honesty is the key factor. I have made this very clear to Ali, so he is quite aware of it. Even knowing this, he holds back when sharing his feelings with me. I was surprised when he opened up about Palar. I guess he saw how pissed off I was that he hadn't told me about her. But there are still other issues, including the incident with Brina; and that thing about his boys still bothers me.

And then there are all the other little things that sometimes trouble me about Ali. Like when he goes into a place where there are women, he positions himself so I can't see his face, particularly his eyes. He does the same thing when we're walking down the street. And then when he's surfing the Net and I walk into the room, he often clicks off the screen he's on. What's that all about? And he has to know I'm aware of these sneaky behaviors; but maybe he's not. These things seem little compared with everything else, but to me it's like lying; and there's no such thing, in my opinion, as a little lie. It really makes me wonder what he does when I'm not around.

Then, too, there are his aspirations. Ali is very comfortable with his job, and although he's doing well, he's not interested in moving up. He says the higher up you go, the more time you have to spend at the office. That may be true, but this attitude concerns me. I just can't see staying at the same level too long. I'm about growing professionally and personally. But rather than spending time on furthering himself, Ali prefers to spend as much time as he can with me, Crystal, his boys, and playing soccer. I'm not complaining about the time he spends doing what he enjoys—certainly not the time he spends with me—but I do think he should want to spend more time being productive. That is the biggest problem I've had in my relationship with Ali. Since I have such high regard for myself (or thought I did), it's hard for me to accept less from others. I think he should expect more, and do more, first of all for himself and second for our relationship. I must admit he does bring fun, laughter, and a soulful kind of spirit to our relationship, but that's not enough. Maybe it's me. Maybe my expectations are too high.

In reviewing my journal, I'm slowly coming to the conclusion that I'm trying to force my opinions and expectations on someone else. I can even see where that has happened over and over again in many situations; not just with Ali. It's very hard for me not to—since I am so opinionated, and know it. The review of my journal has been beneficial in several ways. It's made me realize I've been quite judgmental in dealing with Ali and others. Even if the only thing it has done is make me understand that I need to loosen up on my expectations of others, that alone makes this time well spent.

Ife

The next entry I'm gonna read is one of the most important ones for me. December 31, 2002 - *"Another year is ending. Seemed fitting to take some time out today to review what I've confided in you over the last twelve months. I knew many of the entries would be depressing, but having completed my review of my journal, one year of my life, in four hours and sixteen minutes, my spirit is somewhat uplifted. I've gained insights that I know will help me make several decisions; the main one being my future with Ali.*

I'd already begun to question my relationship with Ali. There is no doubt in my heart that I love him, but I'm not happy about the way he shares information, or should I say, doesn't share information. I can handle a lot of things, but that's not one of them. Although Ali and I have had a couple of conversations about this, I now believe that he just isn't capable of opening up and sharing his feelings, at least, not now or, maybe, not with me. It could be a man thing, or maybe even a Jamaican thing. Either way, I accept there's nothing I can do to change him. Another thing I can't change is the fact that he shows no signs of becoming a go-getter. The more I write, and the more I reflect on the truth that my journal pages tell me, the more I'm convinced that Ali and I just aren't soul mates. This is much too painful to contemplate. Although I accept the truth of this statement and know it will most likely lead to a positive resolution for both of us, I have a feeling my real troubles are just about to begin, not end! I'm calling a travel agent now. I'm going somewhere to chill.

Last month I took my second trip to St. Maarten alone. It was the loneliest time of my life. I spent several hours on the beach before sunset every day, just thinking. The sound of the waves and the most breath-taking view of sunsets I've even seen provided unadulterated solace. This daily treat, on an otherwise agonizing trip, helped me

Cancer *of the* Spirit

make the most painful, but probably the best decision of my life—to sever my relationship with Ali. He called me every day to say how much he missed and loved me. That made my decision even more difficult. I haven't told Ali about my decision yet. The thought of not having him in my life is real hard for me. Knowing it's the right decision doesn't make it easier to accept or to say. I'm gonna tell him though. I have to. I hope I won't break down—I know I will. Excuse my tears.

Ife

Chapter Five

Marlana
Age: 47 - Wilmington, DE

Listening to you, Ena, my heart goes out to you. Relationships with others—having a human connection—is so essential to life; yet it sometimes seems those same life enhancing relationships are exactly what make life so very difficult. I know you'll make the best decision and your confidence will see you through. I know the power of confidence because I lacked it for so long. In fact, insecurity stemming from a feeling of being abandoned—much like Helen—plagued me for many years. I overcame it by forcing myself daily, sometimes minute-by-minute, to act confident, even when I didn't feel that way. Like, now. I'm as nervous as I can be. Speaking in front of a group, no matter how small, frightens me. I'm afraid I will say something off the wall, although that's never happened. Everyone tells me what a good speaker I am. At one time I thought they were just humoring me, but this last year, I've started to believe them. So I know I can do this.

Cancer *of the* Spirit

It was about this time last year when I realized I had overcome my self-doubt. Before that, if I was in a group discussion I would get very combative with "whomever" disagreed with my position or stand on any particular issue. I can honestly say, I didn't discriminate—I would argue anybody down! With the help of my family and a few honest friends who were often puzzled by my behavior, I have really gained quite a bit of insight about myself over the last two years. I've grown quite a bit, although it's been a grueling experience.

I was born 47 years ago in a very small southern town, Honea Path, in South Carolina. Since I was born at home, my birth was kind of a family affair. At the time, my father and mother were living in my grandmother's house - my mother's mother. To this day, my oldest sister, Tina, sometimes tells the story of how she was so worried about my birth because she did not understand what was happening. All she knew was that our mother was distressed, and was not having a pleasant experience.

I am the third of three children born to John Henry and Lois Langford. I have been told that I was a beautiful and healthy baby, unlike my brother, Edgar, who was a beautiful baby too, but contracted double pneumonia a couple of days after he was born. My father literally saved his life by putting together an oxygen tent; something he figured out from his observations in the small town hospital where he had worked as an orderly for many years. The story has become something of a family legend, but a true legend, which I have learned about from his retelling of the story at family gatherings over the years. Even though Papa worked in the town hospital, his own son couldn't be treated there because of segregation. But on top of that, my folks probably couldn't afford the expense of a hospital stay anyway and there was no such thing as health insurance for them. Plus the closest "colored" hospital was a long way away. What I've always remembered about the story was how Papa took stuff from around the house, along with a couple of items he "liberated" from the hospital, and put that contraption together. Who would think that four long pieces of lumber, a large piece of canvas and a short rubber hose could be used to save a life? But it worked.

So as you can see, although my father was not an educated man, he was a very intelligent and talented man. My Papa was a gifted painter and he also did something that was referred to as "constructions"— using everyday items to create whimsical combinations of unrelated objects. He might take a toy car, a Popsicle stick, a plastic plate, a painted clothes pin and small toys—an animal or a soldier, for example—and combine them with natural objects like shells and small sticks. His work might be categorized as "folk art" today. Had his art had been discovered by some rich art patron, I'd be on easy street today.

"I know that's right, Marlana," Leesha says.

But we all believe to this day that making that oxygen tent saved Edgar's life and was a reflection, like his art, of Papa's real genius for making something out of nothing.

Shortly after my birth, my parents moved to Franklin, Tennessee, where my mother's sister, Aunt Hattie Mae, who is here with me, and her second husband, Uncle James, lived. Mama and Papa lived in Franklin until I was four years old. Like most Black folk back then, Mama and Papa worked extremely hard, but neither of their jobs paid very much, so my father worked as a part-time blacksmith—using skills he learned from his uncle—for a well-established white family who owned a horse farm. My mother worked as a maid. To make ends meet, and have a little extra money, they baked delicious apple, blueberry and blackberry pies and sold them on the old beat-up bus that they, and many of the other laborers, rode to get to work every day. Right now, talking about it, I can almost smell those luscious aromas, taste the raw pie crust and see Mama in her red plaid apron with flour on her face and hands. Even though I was young, these memories come back to me very vividly.

Because Mama and Papa wanted us to have a much better life than they had, they decided to migrate north to Philadelphia. They were also determined to escape the stagnation in Tennessee. Looking back, I never felt so alone and uneasy until after that move. Tina and Edgar were school age when Mama and Papa moved, so they took them along. I wasn't old enough to go to school, so, they left me behind with Aunt Hattie Mae. I was very young, but I still remember being extremely upset when they left. I remember kicking and screaming until I was exhausted. But thank you for keeping me, Aunt Hattie Mae.

"You know I love you, girl," says Hattie Mae.

I love you, too, Aunt Hattie. I believed that I would never see Mama, Papa, Tina and Edgar again. I can still recall how scared I was. Before leaving, Mama tried to explain to me—as best she could—how she and Papa had to find a place to live, find work and get my sister and brother enrolled in school. As to be expected of a four year old, I just didn't comprehend it all. I clearly remember thinking that Papa and Mama didn't like me anymore and that's why they didn't take me with them. I think my reaction to so many things in life has been rooted in that deep seated feeling.

It took Mama and Papa six months to get settled in. They immediately returned to Franklin to get me, but by then, the damage to my young spirit had already been done. Until about a year and a half ago, the nagging feelings of uncertainty and anxiety that surfaced during that period of "abandoment" appeared in my life over and over again.

The last time I remember any conscious feelings of insecurity was about three years ago. It was during a very serious conversation with my husband. We had been married for twenty-four years at the time. The topic of conversation was Mama. I get so uptight and emotional when I think about her situation now. I question whether I'm doing the right thing by keeping her at home with me instead of moving her to a long-term care facility where she will have 'round-the-clock care. Sometimes I think I'm inadequate as a caregiver, but I do the best I can. I don't want to put Mama in any facility—and just leave her there. I hope Mama's care is up to par. I hope what I'm doing is ok.

Mama, who is eighty-seven came to live with Akil and me, our son, Sekou, and our daughter, Makina, eight years ago because she could no longer take care of her small four bedroom row house, nor herself. She had begun to leave food burning on the stove and doors unlocked—day and night. Several months prior to moving in with Akil and me, my sisters and I started preparing Mama mentally for the move. It was a difficult transition for her because she had always been so darn independent and still thought she was capable of living alone. Papa had died about two years before she moved in with us. After his death, Mama really began to decline—both physically and mentally. They had been together for fifty-four years, and were true companions—they did everything together. I know she missed caring for him and, after his death, felt she no longer had a real purpose. This thought always brings tears to my eyes.

The original plan was for Mama to move in with Edgar and his wife, Gladys. Mama, Edgar and his family have always been very close. At the last minute Edgar told me that Mama couldn't come to live with he and Gladys because some touchy situation had evolved between them. I could see that he felt guilty, but he said he nor Gladys, could give Mama the attention she rightly deserved. Mama was so disappointed. When they told her, I could see the hurt written all over her face. That was a real sad day for her.

Although Mama's moving in with us was totally unexpected, Akil and my children were very open and accepting of it.

Since she's been with us, both Mama's physical and mental health have continued to decline—and recently, at a much more rapid pace with the onset of dementia. I really have my hands full now! Then a couple of months ago, she got a nasty ugly sore on the heel of her left foot. It just wouldn't heal. She has been a diabetic for many years, but has never had to take insulin shots. She's always taken oral medications. The sore got worse and worse, so Mama ended up having surgery on her foot. The circulation was so poor that gangrene could have begun to set in. Surgery became absolutely necessary; otherwise Mama would have lost her foot, and possibly a part of her leg.

Our family was very reluctant for Mama to have the surgery—mainly because of her age. Her doctors were truthful about the risks involved, but seemed very optimistic that her long-term health outlook would be much better if she had the surgery. We finally agreed to the surgery. Mama's vein transfer surgery was a tremendous success; so successful that the expected follow-up surgery on Mama's foot was not necessary. The surgery corrected her circulation problem, and the sore on her foot has healed on its own.

Mama's lengthy hospital stay and subsequent rehabilitation took its toll on me. I refused to allow her to go to a nursing home for six weeks of rehabilitation, so she came home after her hospital stay. There were

Ife

so many things that had to be done to take care of Mama. I had to get a hospital bed, a stair lift installed, a motorized recliner chair, and all kinds of other supplies. But the one thing that I had the most anxiety about, was administering Mama's medication intravenously, and showing her daytime caregivers how to do the same. I got through it just fine; praise the Lord.

Before Mama had surgery, she was able to do quite a few things for herself, including getting up at night to go to the bathroom. Since her surgery, she has difficulty going to the bathroom alone, dressing and undressing herself, bathing herself, or even walking without someone being by her side. I'm so afraid she may fall. All she needs is a broken hip. Talk about complicating life—Mama's and mine. Although I know Mama is getting excellent care being with me, I know I won't be able to take care of her indefinitely. I am physically and mentally drained, and really don't have a life outside of taking care of her, and my job. This has put a strain on my relationship with Akil, the kids and the rest of my family. It gets very rough sometimes.

Before Mama was hospitalized, she sometimes stayed with Tina and her husband, who live in Virginia. She would stay with them for two or three weeks at a time—usually every five or six weeks. This was an enormous help to me. She can't go to Virginia anymore. Her physical condition has deteriorated to the point that she can't travel that far. Even if she could, Tina does not have the equipment necessary to keep Mama comfortable during her stay. I guess she could get it, though. Tina comes to help out when she can. But realistically speaking, she has a life in Virginia. She also has a disability of her own that restricts her physical capacity to help Mama when strenuous activity is required. I really miss the reprieve that Mama's trips to Virginia gave me. I also miss spending quality time with Akil, and—when they are around—Sekou and Makina. You know how young people are—always on the go.

I think deep down, the situation with Mama causes Akil some anxiety, too. I know he misses driving to the shore or mountains on the spur of the moment, or just having a romantic weekend at home.

Akil, like Mama, is a lover of the outdoors and nature. Both of us enjoyed those weekend trips so much. Akil would never be bothered by Mama's staying with us. He has a true Afrocentric mind-set when it comes to old folks, that is—respect for and reverence of our elders, as he would call them.

I never realized how taking care of a loved one could be so hard on a marriage. It's certainly more than a notion. I sometimes feel that Akil and I are growing apart. I spend most of my time after work and on the weekends caring for Mama. Akil doesn't seem to resent the time I spend with Mama, but I'm not sure.

Although my brother Edgar lives much closer to me than Tina does, he spends very little time with Mama. He and Gladys used to come to get Mama for dinner and overnight visits every once in a while. Once Mama got to the point where she needed a lot of assistance, they stopped getting her. Their children love Mama and have told me how much they miss her. Gladys does prepare special meals for Mama—because of her diabetes. This avoids my having to cook too, when I get home from work. This is a real blessing. Gladys usually brings enough food to last for a week. This has freed me up evenings to relax a little. I've decided to accept whatever assistance I can get from Edgar and Tina, and be thankful for it. Some caretakers don't have any help.

My cousin Sybil, Aunt Hattie Mae's daughter, is a good example of someone who doesn't have any help. Aunt Hattie Mae can tell you.

Ife

She still lives in Tennessee, but is now living with Sybil, her only child. She moved in with Sybil shortly after Uncle Jake, her fourth husband, died last year. After his death, Aunt Hattie Mae had a couple of bad falls. Sybil and I tease her about drinking a lot more Harvey's Bristol Cream now. We jokingly ask her if that's how she is coping with Uncle Jake's death. Right, Aunt Hattie Mae? Sybil, and very reluctantly, Aunt Hattie Mae, agreed that it would be best for her to move in with Sybil.

The move has caused a great deal of stress and unhappiness for my aunt, who, by the way, is still *very* physically fit and strong-willed—as you can see.

Hattie Mae yells out, "It sho has done dat."

Aunt Hattie Mae is most unhappy about having to give up her home and her freedom, as well as most of the things that she and Jake Palmer worked so hard to get. Sybil didn't have any room in her small place to put any of Aunt Hattie Mae's beautiful and bulky furniture, so most of it was given away. I got a few things that she wanted me to have—things that Sybil can have if she ever wants them.

Once in a while, Aunt Hattie Mae acknowledges that her move has been equally as stressful for Sybil, who has lived alone for over twenty years and who is accustomed to doing things her way—the only right way—to hear Sybil tell it.

"Amen, girl," Hattie Mae mumbles.

Since Aunt Hattie Mae doesn't have any other children, Sybil rarely gets a break. Sybil doesn't think that it's a healthy or happy environment for either of them. She's looking into other options—options that will be beneficial to both of them. I know things will get better for Sybil and Aunt Hattie Mae.

"I thinks so, too," agrees Hattie Mae.

Mama and Aunt Hattie Mae have a brother, Oscar, who lives in Delaware. Mama asks about him and Aunt Hattie Mae almost every day. Uncle Oscar has suffered with dementia for many, many years, but has been well taken care of by his loving and devoted wife of over fifty years. Mama's onset of dementia has occurred within the last five years. It is getting progressively worse for her and Uncle Oscar.

Uncle Oscar was recently rushed to the hospital with stomach problems. He had to have emergency surgery, but came through it as physically strong as ever. That seems to run in the family. Good genes, I guess. I think I'll take Mama to see Uncle Oscar soon.

It's quite hard for me to watch the continuous decline in Mama. She rarely remembers what is said from one minute to the next now. Most of the time she doesn't really know who I am. I think she does know that I am someone who loves her and who she can totally trust. She seems to know who Akil is all of the time. That's strange, isn't it? On whatever level she is functioning, I think she knows that she will be cared for and kept safe—out of harm's way. I hope this gives her a sense of security—something, until recently, I blamed her for taking away from me when I was a kid.

I think that feeling secure is so important for Mama. She is often in the middle of a sentence and can't remember what she was going to say. She gets so frustrated. I can see her eyes pleading for help that I can't give her. It crushes my soul. On those rare occasions when we can't get her to the bathroom before she wets herself, I have seen the humiliation that comes over her. I can tell that incidents like that are very painful for her. Our family has learned not to make a big deal over the increasing number of incidents that could take away so much of

Ife

Mama's dignity. For instance, she is still very conscious about having the bathroom door completely closed, even though someone has to be in there to help her. When she was in the hospital, she preferred that the female nurses get her ready for bed. She let it be known too. She is really something. Mama's such a kind and pleasant person, and is still aware enough, much of the time, to be concerned about not being a burden to anyone. My heart gets so full.

Mama does have her trying times, though. She sometimes gets so flustered and sad about no longer being able to do for herself or communicate her feelings, and, most of all, having to depend on someone else for everything. If any of you are going through a similar experience, you're definitely not alone.

I'm real grateful for the evolving resolutions to challenges that I have faced—particularly the ones associated with Mama's declining mental and physical conditions, and my role as her primary caregiver. Several of the solutions to Mama's challenges have primarily come from what I have read. There are so many helpful guides addressing the care of persons with Alzheimer's disease, illnesses related to dementia and memory loss in later life. These guides have been of immense assistance to me. I guess that's enough about Mama for now. My heart goes out to her.

Other pressing issues of insecurity, including concern about my family's financial future and concern about Sekou and where he is headed, still bother me to some extent; but not nearly as much as they did last year.

The insecurity I feel regarding our financial future is not without reason. Akil, who changed his name from Eric about fifteen years ago, is a righteous man. I met him when we were in junior high school and started dating him once we got to high school. He was such a nice guy. He was very popular, mainly because he was the star football player, but also because he was a college prep honor student. Since I was a cheerleader, we often got a chance to see each other after school, during football and pep squad practice.

After high school, we both attended Auburn State College, but only for one year. We were married after that year. I have since completed college and received a Masters degree, and am thinking about getting a Ph.D. in Education. Although I have always been extremely interested in education, at one time I thought the main reason I decided to get my Masters degree stemmed from my feelings about myself not quite measuring up. Feelings that I'm convinced were born that day Mama and Papa left me. Even though I am the best curriculum person in my school district, and know it, I still felt somewhat uneasy and insecure around my Masters and Ph.D. colleagues. Although, I must say, these feelings have drastically changed over the last year. Sometimes I wonder if I've become a little arrogant about my abilities. No....... I don't think so.

OK, OK, stop laughing!!

My free-spirited partner is very creative, self-educated, and very intelligent. During our marriage, Akil has done so many creative things. He has written an exciting novel, which I have encouraged him to have published; painted dozens of masterful pieces; and developed and launched a successful educational program that encourages Black people, particularly our youth, to study and learn more about their history. However, his greatest gift is that of an artist. He's outstanding!

I have always been very supportive of Akil's endeavors, and have personally been involved in many of them. I have been the primary wage earner in our family while Akil has painted and put together projects that I have always felt will eventually generate just as much, or more, as my income. I give him a lot of credit because he always has a regular job when he is working on his side projects. He believes in taking jobs that make some difference in the lives of our people. He has pretty much been able to land that kind of work, although it didn't always pay as much as we would have liked. At times, being the main source of income has been stressful.

When our daughter, Makina, was accepted to Bennett College in North Carolina, I was so happy, but a little worried and stressed out at the same time. I wondered how we were going to pay her tuition. She received a small scholarship, but it was not even enough to cover the cost of her books for the year. Makina has always been so easy-going and considerate. From the time that she was a baby, she has never given us one bit of trouble. She worried that going to college was a hardship for us. Akil hadn't had any success as an artist, or should I say, success getting paid what he should have been paid for his paintings. He knew how badly we needed money for Makina's tuition, so he contacted several school districts about the educational program that he had previously proposed to them. A couple officials had reviewed it and were extremely interested. They told him that as soon as their budgets were approved, they would purchase a substantial number of the books—a companion component of the program—for the schools that fell under their jurisdiction. It took several months before Akil received the purchase orders and then checks, but they did come.

About a month before receiving the purchase orders, his paintings began to sell real well, too. Akil appears so low-keyed, and seemingly unconcerned about our financial situation. I get so down about this. He has told me over and over again that everything will work out—and things finally have. He's always had a great deal of confidence in his ability; especially as an artist.

My confidence and support in Akil are really paying off now. He has sold some of his more expensive paintings to a couple of his high school buddies who have since become star athletes. Their word-of-mouth praise about his paintings has helped him gain a growing clientele and a lucrative business.

When Akil first started selling to "prosperous" clients, we owned a house in the heart of a Philadelphia ghetto. That really bothered me. Talking about feeling insecure. You just don't know. Nightly gun shots, constant and loud music—that roared from cars speeding through the neighborhood—and the constant presence of drug dealers on every corner were scary. Since most of the people in our neighborhood knew Akil, either through his work on the Board of Education, or his local political presence, he didn't feel nearly as threatened or alarmed by the goings-on as I did. Thank goodness Akil's success as an artist has now allowed us to move into a fairly new four-bedroom house. He likes the kitchen the most. He is a great cook, too. He cooks a lot. I love—and appreciate—that. He's so creative in the kitchen. "Creativity" is his middle name. Don't get me wrong, I can cook, too, but Akil 'burns' much better than I do.

Mama's living with us in our new house has become much more pleasant for her. The house is in a beautiful area of Delaware, and has a large deck that overlooks a wooded area. Mama now sits outside and enjoys nature again. She loves being outdoors and missed that at our Philadelphia house. Her old house had a nice back pouch and yard, where she and Papa grew beautiful flowers and plants.

Ife

I'm so relieved and happy to be out of Philadelphia. Somehow, and I don't know why, our move to Delaware caused me to vividly recall the negative affect that moving to Philadelphia from Tennessee had on me. The circumstances of the moves were so different. I'm convinced that my family's move from Philadelphia, made possible by Akil's success, was the beginning of the healing of my inner spirit. I'm feeling a lot better nowadays. For the longest, I hadn't been able to get many of the things—material things—that I wanted and I felt I deserved.

About six months after our move to Delaware, a local art gallery—kind of upscale —offered to display Akil's paintings. He was hesitant at first becuase he likes selling his paintings himself. He especially enjoys interacting with the people who buy them. Because he has always made his sales that way, his paintings have never sold as fast as they could. We're in a new home now, and Akil knows he needs to sell more. Since he is so non-materialistic, I'm surprised at how much he seems to be enjoying our new home. I think he even accepted the reality that both of us have to have a decent income—something that we can depend on—if we want to continue to enjoy a comfortable lifestyle. He did eventually, but reluctantly agree to place his paintings in the gallery. Sales have skyrocketed and made a big difference in the way we live.

Another challenge is with Sekou. He is two years older than Makina. He's going through some things. Like his dad, Akil, he was a star football player in high school. Unlike his father, Sekou and the other star players were pretty much handed everything on a silver platter; and some of them became accustomed to that. Since Sekou was the first child, he was also spoiled—there's nothing unusual about that. Once he finished high school, the combination of his popularity and being spoiled, hindered him from setting and accomplishing any goals. He is a talented writer—like his father—and was, at one point, interested in writing science fiction novels. He received several prestigious awards in high school for outstanding pieces that he wrote.

About a year after graduation, with a big push from Akil and me, Sekou took several writing courses that we thought would help prepare him to write novels, something he said he wanted to do. We just wanted to be sure that he had some hands-on writing experience and formal knowledge about writing styles and techniques. Three and a half years later, there was still very little progress with Sekou's novel writing. It finally dawned on me that novel writing was not for him when Sekou started writing one song after another. During this last year, Sekou's writing ability has really paid off. He has written two songs which, amazingly, have been on Music List's Top 10. He's still doing what he loves—writing—but has focused on something he wants to do, not something someone else wants him to do, namely us. He loves the music industry, and is doing well in it. He's finally willing to put the time and effort into his work.

I'm feeling so much more optimistic and comfortable about a number of things that used to stress me out. Sometimes you don't realize what a negative impact a certain situation has on you until it's no longer an issue in your life. Akil's and Sekou's successes have really eased my mind. Mama is still my biggest concern now.

Extensive talk therapy—that's what I call it—with my immediate family, other close family members and good friends, has helped me accept the possibility that most of my feelings of insecurity were caused by things that I didn't have any control over. Now, when situations occur that cause me to doubt myself, I've learned to lean on the Lord first. I know accepting the Lord as my personal savoir many years ago has gotten me through many trying times. I've also learned to look within. These two saving graces alone have proven very effective for easing or erasing many of my doubts.

I also think I've come to understand the reasons and motivations for Akil's and Sekou's past behaviors. I've concluded they were probably doing some soul-searching themselves. I've especially gained insight into why Akil has put so much effort into painting—or I think I have. His real interest in the freedom of our people—not the counterfeit freedom that we've come to know and accept—is portrayed in all of his works. I think he feels the paintings are the most meaningful way for him to make a statement to the people and the Black community. I'm happy that his paintings are so popular. Financially, we are doing well. His income far exceeds mine now. I'm also thankful for that.

I have talked with Mama, in detail, about leaving me in Tennessee when I was so young. I told her what a negative impact leaving me with Aunt Hattie Mae has had on me over the years. I expressed my ongoing feelings of insecurity, and how those feelings had driven me to excel beyond anyone's expectations—even my own—in almost everything I do. When I was talking with Mama, it hit me like a bolt of lightning that my uncompromising sense of duty to my family, my job and to Mama, had often covered up, and compensated for, my feelings of insecurity. Although I knew Mama's mental state didn't allow her to fully under-stand all that I was saying to her, I had to say it. It was more for me than it was for her. I'm glad she was alert enough to say that leaving me with her sister was out of necessity, and nothing more. She said, "I love you, Marlana." After all of these years, I knew these were the words I had longed to hear. They made me feel fully loved, especially since I'd never heard Mama say, "I love you" to anyone else. Sorry, I can't talk any more.

Chapter Six

Hattie Mae
Age: 79 - Franklin, TN

Marlana ova here tryin to git me to talk bout my life like it were somethin special. It warn't. I had me some good times and I had me some good mens, but I never travel like even little Ena, dare. She been to the Carabeen Islands. I neva been. An I neva got no education to speak of, which always shames me. But still, I done had a good life. All in all, I got nutt'um to complain bout. Well, dats not all the way true. I hate bein ole and not bein on my own, like I's used ta bein. Now I's livin wit my one and only daughter, Sybil. And dat ain't real good fo neither one of us. I's feelin in the way, and she feelin I's in the way. Fo example, when I heared da do'bell ring a month or so ago, I's slowly start walkin to'ards da do' when Sybil come a flyin by me and open it. It was my niece Marlana—sittin right dar—come visitin from Delaware. Sybil had invite huh to have lunch wit us dat day. As always, I's so happy to see Marlana. She done been my favorite niece from da time my sister Lois left huh wid me fo a few months when she was jest a little thang. Po thang, she was

Ife

so scared. I will always have a special place in my heart fo huh. I don' think Sybil has taken too kindly to my likins of Marlana, doe.

Since I's visitin wit Marlana in Delaware now, I's glad I cepted huh invitation to come today—all da way to Texas. I really fears flyin doe, but, here I is.

When Marlana visit Sybil and me in Franklin—and I's so happy Sybil still in Franklin; I loves Franklin, Tennessee—Sybil tells me dat my oder niece, Tina, were carin fo Lois while Marlana were visitin us, cause Marlana care fo my sistah Lois like my Sybil care fo me. I were so grateful fo huh visit.

Like I usually do, while Marlana were visitin wit us, I woke up every mornin wit da sounds of nature comin through my window—birds singin, crickets screamin, and da wind blowin. I start movin bout round six a.m. I heared Sybil grumblin bout me bein wake so early. Huh have never been a early bird, but since I done moved in wit huh, huh have to git up early to fix my brekfus. I can do it myself, but I decide to let someone else wait on me in my old age. I took care of my ailing folks, Della and Frank Madison, by myself til da end of dare lives. Dat warn't too easy fo me. Lois and my brother Oscar was gone from home.

I spect another reason I lets Sybil git up so early is cause I don' feel comtable round huh house. Huh is so pa'ticular bout ever damn thang! It make me nervous round dare. When I first moves in, I tried to do some thangs, but nothing was ever did right, so I quit doin dem. I miss havin my own place. Huh place is so small. I cain't move round witout bumping into somethin. Too much damn stuff in dat house. An ain't none of it mines.

Cancer *of the* Spirit

I move in wid Sybil shortly after my foe'th husband die last year. I reckon I save da best fo last cause Jake Palmer were da love of my life. He were such a kind and lovin man. Jake Palmer treat me mighty good. He always huggin and kissin on me, and tellin me how much he loves bein arounds me. He saids I were the most beautiful creacha he ever see. He buy me pretty thangs all the time and takes me to dem fancy places to eats. He jest die too early. He were only eighty.

Befo Jake die, Sybil remind me dat I had start leavin thangs on da stove til dey burns, leave wader runnin in da tub, and some oder thangs. She say, too, dat since he die, I start drinkin more dan ever to cope wit his death. Mostly based on dose reasons, but maybe fo a few more, Sybil decide I should move in wit huh. I didn' want to, but dare I is. Huh have dem damn peoples to come and take all my thangs. Dat move has cause a great deal of trouble fo me. I's still physical fit and strong-headed; jest a little fogitful at times is all. I must say, I's bitter bout havin to give up my own house, my free movin bout, and most of my thangs dat take me many years of cleanin house fo white peoples to git. I spect dat movin in wit Sybil done been equally hard on huh, too, since huh has lived by huhself fo over twenty years and is used ta doing thangs huh own way—da only right way, to hear huh tell it.

But I feels fo Sybil. Sybil is my onlyest child, so she rarely git a break from me. It ain't a good circumstance fo me or huh. I declare, I sho hope thangs git better. Sybil ofen acts like she ain't got no home trainin a tall.

I overheared Sybil tellin Marlana dat she caught me lookin in da mirror again, and said dat, once again, I seems so taken aback by da way I look nowadays. She say dat cause I don' remember much from day to day, so evertime I look in da mirror is a new sperience fo me.

Ife

Now alldoe I look quite oppsite from da way I done ten or fifteen years ago, I *do* recognize my own face, *an* I think I look mighty good fo my age, seventy-nine. I got so upset wit Sybil when I heared huh talkin bout me. I suppose she think my hearin problem is worser dan it is. I hear some thangs mighty good. Doe sometime Sybil blame me fo hearin only what I wants to hear.

Sybil made a good lunch dat day Marlana come, one of my favorite—roast beef wit gravy, baked potato wit loads of butter and sour cream, brocli and home-made rolls. She even made fresh lemonade, none of dat frozen stuff. To top everthang off, she make a chocolate cake from scratch. I really enjoy my lunch dat day, specially since Marlana were dare. Sometime my lunches wit Sybil ain't so happy. She not da most pleasin thang to be round at times.

After lunch, me, Sybil, and Marlana sit in da livin room and talk bout da good old days. I already had a couple glasses of Harvey Bristol Cream, my favorite drink, wit lunch. An I got another one befo we start talkin. Dat's one thang dat I can do fo myself—git my Harveys. Sybil and Marlana had some of dem Bahama Mama drinks. Huh learned to make dem during one of huh trips to da Bahamas.

All of us felt mighty good by da time dey ask me to tell dem bout my growin up days wit Lois and Oscar on Della and Frank Madison's farm in Woodruff, South Carolina. Dey know I would be able to remember thangs dat happened a long time ago better dan I could thangs dat happened even jest yesterday. Bout six years ago, my memry start to git real bad; funny how I remember dat.

I begin da story by remindin dem dat I was da second child of Della and Frank. He were a carpenter and she were a homemaker. Bof of dem had a real likin fo what dey done. MaMom work hard to make our house a home. Huh know how to do so many thangs good. She was da best cook dat I remember til dis day. She sewed good, too. She sewed almost everthang in our house—curtins, tableclofs, sheets, furniture throws, and all us youngins clothes.

Befo we move in da house dat I remember, MaMom and PaPop was livin in a house on a farm dat dey work da land fo, and make small payments every year to a white man, Mr. Charley. PaPop didn' like workin fo dat white man and said dat he were going to stash enough money away to git his own farm. From da time I first heared him say dat, it take him six years to move us to da house on da farm dat I growed up on. I was ten years old when we move dare. Dat were in 1934. Da house we move in was a spectable size fo a colored family; oder coloreds round us called it da "Big House." It had three sleepin rooms, a good size parlor, eatin room, and kitchen. We had a inside toilet and a washin tub and bowl. MaMom, my sister and brother, and me was so proud of PaPop. We was so happy. Lois and me didn' care dat we had to share a sleepin room. Huh, Oscar, and me had been used ta sleepin in da front room in da house on Mr. Charleys farm. Oscar was glad all of a sudden dat he was da only boy. He had a sleepin room by hisself at our new house.

PaPop had to do a heap of carpentry to da house befo we could move in. Through a little part in da tin roof over da eatin room and da parlor, you could see da sky. PaPop had to fix dose parts first. He also had to fix some of da planks on da floors. They was a might weak. One good thang I remember bout da house was dat it had a icebox in it. PaPop was happy dat he didn' have to buy one. By da time he fixed up all da oder thangs, da money was low. Wit all dat had to be done to da house, we was still excited bout movin to da Madison farm.

Ife

Us youngins went to school two days a week. Da oder foe days we spent workin on da Madison farm. Cause Oscar was a boy, he miss a lot of weeks at school, specially durin da springtime, to help PaPop do some of da heavy thangs dat had to be done. None of us work on da farm on Sunday, cept for feedin the chickens and such. Dat was da day of da Lord, so we went to church and stay dare half of every Sunday. MaMom raise up at five o'clock on Sunday to fix a special brekfus fo us. On da oder days, huh raise up at six o'clock. Dose days we had a ordinary brekfus. Dose was some of da happiest days of my life. God only knows, I wish I could say da same now.

My life seem so empty now. I don' know where my thangs is. Marlana, befo I goes back to Franklin, I wants you to call Sybil and tell huh, I wants my thangs back. Dose peoples come and take them away from me. I git so damn mad sometimes. I feels grateful dat I's wid Sybil, but I feels mad at da same time. I's off da subject, ain't I? Anyways, Ama, I's so happy dat you has some Harveys. One of you youngins, git me another glass, please.

Now, what was I talkin bout? Les see…oh yeah! Anyways, we had a heap of animals on our farm—hogs, cows, chickens, and a couple or two horses. Lois, Oscar, and me was sponsible fo feedin dem most of da time. Marlana, I hope dat you don' mind hearin dis again. We was also sponsible fo takin care of da big garden dat MaMom had dug up and plant corn, cabbage, tomato, green bean, potato, and oder seeds in. Huh always done cannin in da summer and fall to be ready fo winter. Huh want to be sure dat we always eat good.

Da whole family work on our farm fo two solid years. After dat, Lois went off to dat normal school, Stebens-Lee, I thinks. Den Oscar went to da Army in 1937. I was lef on da farm by myself wit PaPop and MaMom. Da year befo Lois and Oscar lef, PaPop taken a fall and hurt his back. From den on he felt poorly, but still forced hisself to work da farm. MaMom and me done as much as we could to help him. MaMom tells him dat he should git some outside help, but he didn' want to. Said he didn' trust nobody.

PaPop got real sick three years after his fall. It got to da point dat he couldn' do no farm work and took to da bed. Doc Jones advise him to git help at dat time. He know MaMom and me couldn' work da farm by ourself, so PaPop gots three brothers from a nearby farm to come help us in dare spare time. Dey did a fair to middlin job when dey wasn' trying to get fresh wid me.

After PaPop got to da point dat he couldn' do nothin fo hisself, MaMom work so hard to take care of him, da house, and da farm, dat huh start ailin, too. Ever since I can remember, she had a mild heart problem. When she was put upon wit all of da sponsibilities of da farm, she started feelin worser and worser. She always liked dat I was around to help huh. I felt resentment to'ards Lois and Oscar cause dey wasn' dare at dat tryin time. Dey was away gittin a education, somethin I never have a chance to git. I needed help dat I didn' have. Til dis day I remember dose times.

PaPop died of some kind of complication a year after he took to da bed. I were fifteen at da time. After his death, MaMom didn' seem to care much bout anythang. It were like witout PaPop, she couldn' make heads or tails of anythang.

Lois and Oscar come home fo PaPops burial. It were only da third time dat dey come home since dey leave. Da oder two was fo holidays. Dey look so different when dey come. All growed up and all. Dey even talk funny. I suppose dat were from gittin educated—Oscar in

Ife

the military and Lois in normal school. I's da one dat had to quit my education to help take care of thangs on da Madison farm. Dat makes me feels so shame til dis very day, not havin a education an all—dats why I didn' wanna talk tonight.

I always sweared dat my chirrun would git a education. Sybil is very learned. She know how to work wit dem computers an all. It make me so damn mad when huh don' let me touch huh computer, doe. I wish she would learn me how to use it. I's off da subject again. I wants another one of dem Harveys, please.

Lois act scared when she see dat MaMom didn' have no color in huh cheeks nor no excitement bout nothin. She want to quit huh last year at normal school and stay home wit me. I tell huh dat I could care fo MaMom and do all da oder thangs dat had to git done. I insist dat huh goes back to school. Huh said she would. Oscar didn' pay no mind to nothin. He act like nothin didn' happen. Mens tries to be strong sometime. I suppose he was hurtin bad insides. He and PaPop was bosom buddies.

When PaPop leave dis earth, MaMoms heart git more weak. Huh lasted fo two years after we burried PaPop. Durin dat last year of MaMoms life, I come to know one of da boys dat come to help us on da farm. Since I was da one to hand out orders when MaMom git too sick to work, I git to know Steve, Allen, and Thomas Keller real good. Thomas were my favorite. After MaMom pass, he talk me in lettin him have his way wit me. I knowed it was wrong cause MaMom done teached me better, but I was alone and I was lonesome, so I done it anyways. I feel shame when it was over. Seem like I was all da time feelin shame bout somethin.

Cancer *of the* Spirit

MaMom tell me and Lois bout not lettin boys have dare ways wit us, but huh never tells us what could happen. So when Doc Jones tell me dat I were spectin a baby, I didn' know what to say, didn' know what to do. He make a home visit cause I were sick every mornin fo a heap of weeks. He ask me what boy had his way wit me, and I tell him. He warn't taken aback like I was. Dat made me feel shame again. He tell me to git word to Thomas Keller right away.

When I tells Thomas bout da baby, his face lit up. He have da biggest smile I ever seen. Fo a minute, I didn' feel shame, but den, I did. Thomas say we should git married right away. Right den, fo some reason, I wonder what was da circumstance of MaMoms and PaPops gittin married. I wish I knowed. I also wish Lois was dare wit me cause huh was older and could tell me what I should do.

Thomas and me git married. Last month was da first time I tells Sybil bout da matter of huh bein born. Huh daddy and me warn't married too long, bout three years. I tells Sybil dat I reckon I done it mainly cause of huh. She were born a healthy seven-pound baby, and huh, Thomas, and me stay on da Madison farm cause I want to. I had done put a heap of hard labor in dat farm and warn't gonna leave it. But Thomas wined up bein one of dem mean mens. I reckon dat's where Sybil gits huh mean self sometimes. I ain't dat way. When I wouldn' put his name on da deed to da farm, da devil in Thomas Keller come out. He raise his hand to me and threaten to hurt me if I didn'.

One day while he was workin, I packs up me and Sybil and leaves fo Tennessee, where some of PaPops first cousins live. Befo I leave da Madison farm, doe, I tells da law to git Thomas away from da farm. Da sheriff was the fairest white man I ever meet. Peoples don' believe me when I tell em dat. Cause most of dem ain't dat way. You knows back in dem days, colored folks got treat bad by the law all da time. I don' mean to hurt nobodys feelin, Miss Dominee. I's jest tellin it like it is. But see, Sheriff Johnson growed up wid PaPop and later on dey was fishin' buddies. He was bout the onliest white man, oder than Abe Lincoln, that PaPop had anything good to say bout. I tells ole Sheriff Johnson bout Thomas bad treatment to'ards me and dat I was goin to Tennessee wit Sybil. I tells him dat I will be back to sell da farm as soon as I get sitiated in Tennessee. I felt guilty bout leavin behind ever-thang PaPop and MaMom work so hard fo—da same dang thang dat happen to me again when I move in wid Sybil.

PaPop's cousins takes me and Sybil in til I could git some farm work. Dats all I knowed how to do. I didn' have no education. It was good dat PaPop teached us young'ns to tuck away some money fo hard times, cause it took me longer dan I expected to git sitiated dare. My cousins didn' know bout nobody havin no farm work for me at da time I gits dare. I were dare fo foe months befo dey heared of anythang. In a hurry, I takes da work dey point me to. It was fo a cook job on da Old Gaston farm.

Da Gastons had a lot of colored folk workin fo dem. Dare farm was so big dat I couldn' see it all wit one look, dey own so much land. Dey seem to be good peoples, too, specially, Ole Lady Gaston. All da col-oreds call dem Ole Man and Ole Lady Gaston. I felt good bout workin fo dem at first. Dose feelins was cut mighty short when Ole Man Gaston approach me in a bad way bout a month after I start cookin. When he saw how scared I looked, doe, he back off me. He didn' come up to me no more. Dat old cracker.

When I goed to Tennessee, I writ, as good as I coulds, some friends of PaPop and MaMom back home. I had ask dem to be lookin round fo anybody wantin to buys da Madison farm. After MaMom died, Lois and Oscar said I could haves da farm cause dey wasn' interested in holdin on to it. I warn't either no mo. I reckon I want to be as far away from da memories of Thomas as I could git.

Bout six months after I had been in Tennessee, I finally got da news dat I had been waitin fo; some more colored folk want to buy da farm. PaPop didn' want no white peoples to git our land. I went back to da Madison farm fo da last time to sell it. When I got there, I seed dat Thomas done moved most everthang out da house. Dat made me mighty mad and sad at da same time. Dat was such a motional time fo me. I remember so many happy times in our house. I was sorry I had to leave cause of bad thangs. It made me feel mighty poorly back den. But dat was way back in 1941. I got a pretty good piece of change from sellin dat old farm, doe. An dat money allow me to buy a decent place of my own fo me and Sybil. Dare are heaps of good memories from Tennessee fo Sybil and me. Marlana, you heared me say dat befo, right? When huh turn sixteen, Sybil leaves my place. Huh gits huhself a job an apartment, and started takin night studies in business. I gotta say my baby got a good head on huh shoulders.

I meets my second husband, James Ackins, in Tennessee. He was a very religious man. I spot him from a distant whiles I were sittin in church one Sunday. I seen him befo, but never paid no tenshun to him. He had a fectious grin. I suppose he musta saw me lookin at him, cause after da sermon was over, he comes up to me outside and tips his hat and speak to me. He never done dat befo. After a little bit of talk, he tips his hat again and say he would see me next Sunday. I felt a little tinglin in my body all week. I knows Sunday was comin soon. Ole Lady Gaston even comment on how happy I seem all dat week. Fo a change, every meal was a pleasin to cook dat week. When I leaves da Gaston farm on dat Saturday evenin, I was so full of joy; Sunday was almost dare.

Ife

James Ackins looked afar mo better dan he did da Sunday befo, all-doe he look good den, too. I was already sittin when he got to church. As soon as he see me, he came right over and plop down next to me. I was bustin wit joy. I knowed dat da Lord had bless me den. Dat were da best church service I ever attend. After da service, James Ackins and me talk again. He ask if he could come callin some evenin in da week. I tells him dat I didn' git home til pitch black. James Ackins end up bein da husband dat Sybil like da most. Wouldn' you know dat he be da one dat die from a stroke a few months after we tie da knot?

It gittin pitch black here, Marlana. We better git ready to go back to your house on da airplane. Where does you live anyways?

"We're not flyin home until tomorrow mornin, Aunt Hattie Mae. We're going to spend the night in the hotel, remember? So we don' have to hurry. Please…I love to hear you talk bout your life. Please go on."

Well, okay. Course, I ain't in dat big of a hurry to get back home anyway—I mean not to Sybil's. Marlana, after you leave our house when you comes fo a visit, Sybil and me goes back to our ole habits—I turns in early every night cause I likes to git up so early, and Sybil cuts huh television on and lets it run all night. Sometimes I cain't sleep too good and I gits up in da middle of da night. I hears huh TV. I reckon dat TV is huh companion; I know I ain't. Sybil seem so lonely at times. Dats when huh really act awful mean. I's lonely, too. I miss Jake Palmer a mighty heap.

Sybil keeps tryin to git me in some kinda program to be wit ole peoples. I ain't ole and don' wanna git in no ole people program. But Sybil says da program would make me feel better. I reckon I could try it; might be dat I don' mine bein wit ole peoples. Might git a chance to go to some parks an be outside, talk and make some thangs, too. Maybe even git to go on trips sometimes. I'd like dat. I might even feel more at home at dat program dan I does at Sybil's. Dats shame to say dat, but it could be da God's truth.

I gits real lonely fo my sister and brother sometime. Alldoe we ain't been livin close fo years, I gits a little jealous cause dey lives so close together. Fo years after James died, dey invite me to come to Delaware fo awhile. After Sybil leave home, I finally took dem up on dare invitation. I wine up stayin in Delaware fo almost thirteen years. Sybil watch over my place while I were dare. She come to Delaware to see me once in awhile when I live dare, but not too ofen. I stay wit Oscar and Gladys fo three years, dat were til I git married again. Does was good days in my life. From time to time, I done some house cleanin to help wit thangs around Oscar house. He and Gladys said I didn' have to, but I want to. Dat were back in 1954.

Da men folk I finds while in Delaware were Lamar Hastings. He is da one dat become husband number three. I reckon I always felt da need fo someone to take care of me, cause in da past I always takes care of someone else. I done had so many last names dat I cain't remember all of dem myself half da time.

Lamar were a kind an gentle man. I met him at da grocery stoe. I drop a can of carnation on da floe and bends over to pick it up when Lamar gits it befo me. I thanks him, and in his soft speech he say I were more dan welcome. He say dat I were wearin a mighty pretty dress. He sho nuf stirs my heart. I reckon I don' have to say dat he asked to see me again, and don' have to say dat I did. Cause I been physical fit all my life, mens all da time likes to eye my body parts. A mighty good part of da time, I could tell what was on dare dirty minds.

Ife

Lamar and me was married a couple of months after we first meet, much to da dislike of Lois, Oscar, and Gladys. Dey said it was too soon fo me to marry a man I jest meet. I didn' pay no mind to what dey said. Lamar Hastings was one of da best thangs dat ever happen to me in my whole life.

I lef out of Oscar house and move in wit Lamar. We live happy in Delaware fo almost ten years. Den Lamar and me bof start feelin poorly. So Lamar and me start talkin bout movin back to my house in Tennessee, where da enviment were better fo us. Sybil were still takin good care of my house dare, cause she know I would come back one day—dats what I tells huh.

By da time me and Lamar move, I was real ready to be back in Tennessee. It feel so funny to be back in my house again. Sybil had took real good care of it. I let huh know how much I appreciate it. Like me, Sybil done take a husband while I were in Delaware. Dey marry bout six years after I leave Tennessee. She seem very happy wit huh husband, Herman, in da beginnin. He was a real hard worker and plain ole nice man. Dey live in Sybil's ole place, a two sleepin room apartment. Sybil all da time want a house, and be puttin pressure on Herman to git dem one. Herman were very comtable livin wit Sybil in dat nice apartment, but Sybil want a place wit more space. They stay at my house alot cause of dat. Huh think dey would have chirrun some day. But dey didn' never move, an neither did dey have any youngins. Sybil was too impatient den—still is now. Huh pressurin him fo a house an chirrun jest got on his nerves. Dat what I think anyways. He jest got tied of huh foolishness and lef. Dey still good friends doe. It such a shame.

Cancer *of the* Spirit

Sybil start gittin real mean bout five years after Herman leave, an got worser over da years. My baby's such a bafflement to me. Huh was such a warm child. Fo da life of me, I don' know what happen to huh. Lord knows I catches hell now. I suppose she do, too. We is some match!

I was wit Lamar Hastings fo twenty-eight years; da most I was wit any one man. But to'ads the end, I could feel myself gittin a might antsy, specially since I had saw Jake Palmer again when I goed back to Tennessee. I'd knowed him from many years back. Befo I lef Tennessee to go to Delaware, he approach me a lot, even doe I was married. I knowed he was testin my will, an Lord, he sho were a test! But den I up an lef Tennessee an meet Lamar. Me an Lamar had a real good life together, until I got back to Tennessee, den he got so demandin on me, and jealous of anybody I seen, or even talk wit. I been a good wife, all da times doin what he say and followin all his decision. I never made any fo my ownself. I kept his favorite food on da table, and kept everthang round da house spic'n span. But once we got to Tennessee, I couldn' do nothin by myself no mo. I didn' know what had come ova him. Demons, I suppose! I said to myself, "He better look at hisself real hard and change his ugly ways, else here comes husband number foe, Jake Palmer." Mens sho do calm my soul!

Dat's my story; an all dat talk made me a might thirsty. Ama, you got any Harveys lef? Let me have one mo for the road. I's ready to go home, Marlana.

"Aunt Hattie Mae, remember that our home tonight is that nice hotel just up the street. But you are certainly right. It is time—oh my goodness, look at the time!—to go. I had no idea it was so late. We'll see y'all in the morning."

Ife

Ama agrees, "Ladies, that's it for tonight. I'm about through. I'll have some breakfast for you in the morning. I won't be mad if a couple of you want to help."

*   *   *   *   *   *

With some hesitation in her voice, Sharon says, "Ama, you know I was thinking—if the other ladies don't mind—I could take the tapes that you're making, transcribe them, and put together a compilation of our stories. As an aspiring writer, I would love to take this on as a project."

"Miss Sharon, I think that's a wonderful idea. I'm honored by the thought. It will be a real tribute to Ma—something that can be passed on to future generations, too. And come to think of it, the lessons of these stories can be used for my youth project as well. Ladies, think about it and let me know at breakfast, OK?"

Chapter Seven

Alicia (Leesha)
Age: 60 - Alexandria, VA

The doorbell rings at eight-thirty a.m. Ama says to Ena, " I know that's Makeba. That girl does not believe in going any-where late." When Ama opens the door, she yells, "I told you." With a big smile on her face, Makeba steps in. " Good morning, Ama. It's smelling real good up in here. Those rolls were delicious yesterday. I'm sure glad some are left."

"There weren't, girl—I'm making some more—one of Ma's favorite recipes. Come on in, Makeba. Ena and I can use your help."

By nine-thirty, everyone has arrived. Hattie Mae comes in saying, "I's hungry as a horse. Is it time to eat?" "Yes, it certainly is" whispers Ama, as she directs her to the head of the table.

Once everyone is seated, Ama says, "Before we get going today, I want to know did all of you think about taking Miss Sharon up on her offer to document this weekend?

Ife

"I did, and think it is a wonderful idea," remarks Catherine.

"Me too," says Ena in a soft and serious voice.

"Ditto," shouts Leesha.

"I guess we're all in agreement then. Is that right?" asks Ama.

In unison, everyone shouts, "that's right"—except Hattie Mae. Her mouth is full.

As each woman finishes eating, she goes into the living room. When Leesha finishes, she goes into the kitchen with a hand full of dirty dishes. Ama calls to her, "Miss Leesha, we'll do those dishes later."

"All right," responds Leesha.

Dominique reminds Leesha, "You started to say something last night—or should I say early this morning. What was it?"

*   *   *   *   *   *

I would have to be the one to follow Miss Hattie Mae's performance last night. Hattie Mae, you may think your life is nothing special, but, Lady, I find you fascinating. And I love your sense of humor. I can only hope you and your daughter find some middle-ground for peace, and that she can find someone to love her, 'cause you know that's all she needs. I, for one, greatly appreciate you sharing your life with us. As far as men being calming—knowing what I know of my life and after listening to the other stories today—all I can say is, you, Hattie Mae, have got to be the *luckiest* woman on Earth. Seriously, though, and to be honest, I have known a few good men, but, God knows, I have also known the worst.

Cancer *of the* Spirit

So let me begin by saying that it was that last beating that made me take a serious look at my life. Not only did Larry attack me, but for the third time he went after our boys who were trying to protect me again.

Until that cold winter night, I had suffered through four years of mental and physical abuse from Larry. It wasn't until he started abusing our boys that I decided to do something about it. I was tired of packing them up in the middle of the night and going to the shelter for safekeeping. My boys were such great kids. In fact it was when they started trying to protect me from Larry that he started beating them, too. I had to do something. The cops had come to know the Kenton family very well, having to come to our place sometimes a couple of times a month only to have me not press charges. They became very annoyed with me. I can't say that I blame them. So imagine their surprise, especially Officer MacIntosh's, that last time. Larry had started slapping me around again, and the boys tried to stop him. Unbeknownst to me, my seven year old, Robert, had already dialed 911 when I headed for the phone to call the cops. Before I could pick up the receiver, I heard that thunderous knock at the door and opened it to find Officer MacIntosh standing there. He always seemed to be on duty when the beatings occurred. Once again he asked, "Mrs. Kenton, when are you going to stop dropping charges and do something about this craziness?"

"Right now, Officer MacIntosh!" I *finally* pressed charges. Larry pleaded, "Leesha, baby, please don't have me locked up," as they led him away. Our boys were nine, eight, seven, and six when Larry went to jail. We all sat down on the floor and cried.

Ife

The judge gave him a sentence of a mere two and half to three years for spousal and child abuse, but Larry's temper did for us what that judge would not—it added seven years to his sentence. Larry got into a fight with another prisoner and killed the man. I thought a two and a half year sentence was ridiculous anyway so I was glad that his time was extended, although I was sorry that it was because he had killed a man.

I was sixteen and pregnant with Noel, our first child, when we stood in front of that justice of the peace and got married; but it wasn't until after Lloyd, our fourth son, was born that the beatings began. Until then we were a happy little family. At seventeen, Larry had been fortunate enough to get a job as an electrician's assistant. He seemed to have a knack for the work and got nice pay increases each of the three years he was with Electrical Power. He was expecting another raise when the company began to falter and lay off workers in large numbers. Larry wasn't in the first group to go, but it wasn't long after the first layoff that the second one followed. Larry was in that group. He was very angry but started looking for work immediately. Everyday he went out looking but couldn't find anything. The trouble began a few months after his lay-off. The longer he was unemployed, the more unbearable he became. A few of the stories Larry had told me shortly after we got married about his childhood gave me the impression that he'd had a violent temper growing up. Well, he'd done an excellent job of keeping it under control—at first.

The stress of not having a job put Larry's life in turmoil and he soon began taking it out on me. I couldn't do anything right, and the boys seemed to get on his nerves all the time. Although Larry drew unemployment pay, it wasn't enough to cover all of our bills. I thought about getting a job, but it wouldn't have been worth it for me to work, since we had a four, three, two, and one year old at home. All I would have earned would have gone to a baby-sitter. So, instead, I began babysitting for two neighborhood kids. That really helped our financial situation.

The first time Larry slapped me was a total shock. I had just come back from the grocery store and was putting the food away when he came into the kitchen. He saw a couple of cans of red salmon on the counter. With a real dirty look, he said, "So now you making enough money to buy salmon? Are you trying to prove you can make it without me, huh?" I tried to explain to him it was on sale and was just as cheap as tuna or anything else I would have bought. "Don't tell me that lie! I know the difference in the price of tuna and red salmon," he yelled. He slapped me and left the kitchen in a huff. He hit me so hard I fell against the counter, but he was gone before I could say another word.

I can joke now, but at that time I was so hurt, so bewildered I couldn't even cry. I remember thinking, "This man has really lost his mind." In a way, I felt sorry for him because I knew what he was going through, but, heck, it wasn't my fault. I was just happy that the boys were taking a nap and didn't see it.

The next day Larry and I had a long talk about the incident. He apologized, saying he was so frustrated about not having a job, not having any money in his pocket, and not being able to take me and the boys anywhere. He made me a promise that he would never hit me again. His promise didn't last long. In fact he kept making it and kept breaking it until I had him arrested four years later.

I divorced Larry while he was in prison—about five years into his sentence. He agreed to the divorce, with some reluctance. It didn't come as a surprise to him, though. When he first went to prison, I visited him regularly, but the visits usually didn't go well. By the time he agreed to the divorce, the visits had dropped to only about two a year. I never took the boys; he had brutalized them, and they didn't want to visit him.

Years later, when I heard that Larry was released from prison, a flash of fear went through my body like a flash of lightning, but I didn't let it stop me from living my life. I hoped he wouldn't seek revenge on me and our boys, but I didn't know for sure. Several people from church saw him before the boys and I did. They told me he seemed to be much more together than he was before he went to jail. They said he looked healthy and peaceful. I expected him to call soon after he was released, although our boys, or should I say young men, weren't that excited about seeing him. Larry had been out of their lives for ten years. All they remembered were the horrible beatings. I told them he was still their father, no matter what, but I was sure he didn't expect them to look at him as a loving dad.

Larry finally called and came by. All of us were home. Our reunion was short and cordial. He apologized humbly for the way he had treated us, and said he wished things had been different. He also said that he had read many motivational books while he was in prison, and was going to try to live a better life. I'll never forget that he joked about having been a "loyal and long-time consumer of correctional services." That provided a welcome tension breaker. We haven't seen him since that night, twenty-five years ago. One of Larry's old high school buddies told me that he left town. I will be a divorced woman of thirty years in June. Incredible!

Cancer *of the* Spirit

I realized recently that for over half of my life, I was out of touch with my true spirit. There were two periods—the four years my boys and I were mentally and physically abused by Larry, and the thirty years of loneliness from not having a good man by my side; someone in my life to share my deepest feelings, and hopes and dreams.

My boys kept me going over the years, though. Being a single parent was a challenging, and rewarding endeavor. I was lucky my sons listened to me and did as I asked and expected, and they were always good students. That's not to say they were angels, by any means. They got into their share of trouble, but they were the type of boys that girls write home about. And they all grew up to be good men. Today all of them are committed to their families and are strong men, determined to be positive role models for their children—and their community. They've always been very active in the church and even today attend church on a regular basis. They're now in their forties. That's unbelievable to me. Three are married and have children of their own, and the forty-three year old, a minister, plans to marry next fall. One of the major programs his church runs assists battered women and children. Clearly our past had a tremendous impact on his soul.

My five grandkids are between five and seventeen, and each is a true delight. I've found that being a grandparent is quite different than being a parent; had I known this from the beginning, I would have just become a grandparent and left the rest alone. Just joking! But truly, my grandkids bring such happiness in my life.

Even with all that, the one thing I missed most over the years was having a long-term, intimate relationship with someone. Several times I got involved with men from my church. That never worked out. I really suspect it had something to do with most men not wanting to get seriously involved with a woman who had a ready-made family, and definitely not with someone who has four *boys*. But even after the boys were on their own, I still couldn't find anyone. Maybe the guys thought I was too old by then, and were looking for someone younger to take care of their tired old behinds.

I did have one relationship after my divorce from Larry. His name was Lou, and while it lasted, I really enjoyed the companionship. I met Lou at the African Art Museum. He was a few years younger than me, around fifty-six when we first met, and liked doing a lot of the things I enjoyed—going to gospel concerts, operas, museums, and book fairs. He was also very virile, so we relished our nights together as much as we did our days.

"I know that's right," says Makeba in a timid whisper.

We saw each other on a regular basis for about ten months when he suddenly got sick. He had to be taken to the hospital, complaining about having a problem "peeing" when he went to the bathroom. He was diagnosed with prostate cancer. That news messed him up so bad he stopped seeing anyone outside of his family, including me.

I was so sorry about his illness. But honestly, I was also upset about the way he chose to handle it. Prostate cancer is a treatable disease when it's caught early enough. I mean I sincerely hope his treatments have gotten rid of the cancer, and he is well again. But I haven't heard. His family is very closed-mouthed about his situation; it's as though they were throwbacks to the 18th century when people were ashamed to admit to having medical problems. I mean it's ridiculous. I finally had a loving relationship that had a real likelihood of growing into something more, and look what happens.

Cancer *of the* Spirit

But the funny thing is, when one door closes, another one opens; and sometimes it's like that game show—what's behind door number three might just knock your socks off. Dwight, the man in my life now, has actually known me for over thirty-five years. But we had only been friends until shortly after the last time I saw Lou. Larry and I had met Dwight and his wife Candice during a National AME Church Conference. We were barely grown at the time. We were among the youngest couples there and we hit it off right away. Every night after the scheduled activities ended, we spent hours together talking and laughing. In fact we spent most of the week-long conference together. That week was the beginning of a close friendship that lasted until Candice's sudden death about seven years ago. She had a heart attack—such a terrible, tragic loss.

Candice and Dwight didn't have any children when we met, although eventually, like Larry and I, Dwight and Candice also had four children. When we met, Larry and I already had two, Noel and Melvin. Candice and Dwight had their first child six years later. By then Larry and I had two more and were already having major problems. I could always count on Candice and Dwight to listen to my tales of woe and offer sensible advice. They even sometimes advised Larry. Both of us really liked them; they were spiritual and kind-hearted and seemed wise beyond their years. Our friendship grew so strong that we became God-parents to one of each others' children. Losing Candice was a horrible loss to me; it was doubly hard on Dwight. It took him many years to even half-way recover from her death. They were still very much in love after all their years of marriage.

After Candice's death, my friendship with Dwight grew. Both of us continued to actively participate in not only our God-children's lives, but our own children's lives as well—although all of them were grown.

Ife

We became a combined family of sorts. Friends have commented on how well our families get along and how happy we all seem with one another. We still see our children often. Of the group of eight, only five have children; three of mine and two of Dwight's.

Dwight's always had a great sense of humor, a lively spirit, and adventurous nature. He's an engineer, but not at all stiff like most of them are. Even at sixty-three years old, he is still quite daring. He's a race car fanatic, and has two cars of his own that he keeps in tip-top condition so he can race at the drop of a hat. I tease him about being too old to be a speed demon. He's spent a lot of weekends at competitions—even won a few. He's also spent thousands of dollars getting his cars ready for those competitions. Did you know that racing cars is one of the most expensive hobbies there is? I went to a couple of the competitions with his kids. I have to admit, they were pretty exciting, but scary. What's also kind of scary is he spends too much money, as far as I'm concerned, betting on other races. He told me that many years ago he had a gambling problem and had racked up a substantial debt from losing so many bets. He says he got help and now that problem is behind him. I hope so.

Dwight's also quite a good skier. At least skiing is something I can relate to. I began taking my boys skiing when they were in their early teens. We're all pretty decent skiers and still look forward to taking our family trip to the Pocono Mountains in Pennsylvania every year. Dwight, Candice, and their children took many of those trips with us.

Well, about ten months ago, Dwight began to send me gifts. He has always sent a card or a little something for my birthday, special holidays, and other occasions like that, but never anything unexpectedly. Each time he sent something, I called to thank him and ask what was up. He'd say, "The gift is just because you're you—a wonderful person—and to say thanks for being such a fantastic God-mother all of these years."

Eight and a half months ago he sent me two-dozen yellow roses. Again, I didn't know what was up, but it made me feel a little uncomfortable. I wanted to talk with him about it, and regardless of what he said, I had planned to make that the last "just for nothing" gift he sent. When I called to thank him and ask him not to send any more gifts, I got the shock of my life. Dwight told me he was sending the gifts to express his true feelings for me, that he had grown to love me in a more-than-family way and wanted us to start dating. I was so shocked I couldn't say anything and almost dropped the phone. He kept saying, "Leesha, are you there? Are you there?" Well, I finally got myself together enough to say "Yes, I am here" and also asked him, "Are *you* all there?"

I *wondered* what was wrong with him and asked him did he know what he was saying. He said he knew *exactly* what he was saying and had finally gotten up enough nerve to tell me what he was feeling. I told him that he needed to come by the house that evening so we could talk about his far-fetched notion. I mean, for goodness sake, he's sixty-three and I'm sixty; we have grandchildren, for crying out loud. I tell you, I wasn't prepared for that conversation, especially over the phone. When I hung up, I literally felt weak, and had to sit down and take a few deep breaths.

Well, Dwight didn't wait until evening to show up. I'd been cleaning the house when I called to thank him for the beautiful roses and was still sitting and thinking about what had happened when he arrived. I wasn't looking my best either. Before he could get through the door, I said, "Dwight, we have been the best of friends for so long, why would you want to ruin that?" He just laughed. We sat down and had a long, long conversation—the conversation that turned my life upside down in a way that I would never have imagined, but now feels so right. Although I had always felt very comfortable and enjoyed being around Dwight, I had never, not once, thought of him as anything other than a good friend. Not until that day.

Dwight and I have now been dating for eight months. It has been quite interesting and a whole lot of fun. We really enjoy each other. Our backgrounds couldn't be more different. Even the way we express things is very different. Candice and I had much more in common. I guess that's to be expected of two women, especially two Black women. Still I have to admit our differences do concern me somewhat. Another thing I'm a little concerned about is Dwight's fanaticism with racing. I still see his racing as a potential problem, and then there's the gambling—I've seen some worrisome signs. We've discussed it several times. But…so far, so good.

About two months ago Dwight asked me to marry him. At that time, I told him I'd give it serious consideration and let him know. The only person I told was my mother, who I have always shared everything with—everything except Larry's abuse. She is eighty years old, but her mind is as sharp as a tack. My mother said, "Girl, you are not getting any younger, and Dwight is an honorable man. Don't let no 'differences' make you silly, and don't let this opportunity pass you by if you make each other happy." I've always listened to her advice. It usually pays off. She was the first one, years ago, to tell me to press charges against Larry once I finally told her he was abusing me and my boys.

Since neither Dwight nor I had mentioned marriage after that first proposal, I think he was surprised when he casually asked again and I immediately said yes. In a way, I'm surprised myself. I mean, for goodness sake, I am a sixty-year old independent Black woman, accustomed to doing things my way. I have made myself content with my single life for thirty years. But then again, it has often been sad and lonesome; I'm really happy about my loneliness coming to an end. I'm looking forward to Dwight and I taking care of each other. Our relationship has really grown, and I care for him much more than I thought I could.

After I said yes, we called all of our children and gave them the news. Despite the fact that the news took some of them off guard, Noel and Robert said they long suspected it and it was about time! All of our children are elated about our marriage.

The wedding's only three months away; and now that it's all real, I'm very excited. And yes, we are going to have a large elaborate wedding. Dwight even wants to be involved in the planning. But can you believe I had no idea of how expensive a wedding could be? Had I known when I first started planning, I may have considered eloping. I'm just kidding; I really do want a big wedding. But I still don't have things as organized as I would like them to be. The woman who's making my dress is having a problem getting the material I chose. We've checked out several nice places for the reception but haven't yet chosen one. Our major concern is the location. We want it to be as convenient and comfortable as possible for our four hundred guests; yes, you heard me, four hundred guests. I hadn't planned on four hundred people though. I was thinking two hundred at the most. Was I wrong, or what! We've tried several times to shave the list, but haven't been successful yet, considering all my friends, all his friends and all of our combined families. And speaking of friends, because Dwight and I have so many good friends, we decided to have only a best man,

Ife

Dwight's older brother, and a matron of honor, my sister, who has lived in California all these years. We didn't want anyone's feelings to be hurt. But time is getting short. We've got to find a place soon.

Dwight's planning our honeymoon, and keeping it a secret. That's fine with me. I love surprises. I hope it's going to be somewhere warm, with a beautiful view of the ocean. He knows what I like, so I know wherever we are going will be superb. Dwight has great taste.

I must say, I haven't been this happy or excited in years. Is it obvious?

"Yes, girl, it is very obvious! You are glowing!" shouts Helen.

Am I? In fact I really can't remember the last time I really felt happy. Anyway, I expect to have the best wedding ever. Even though it's a different kind of excitement, I feel as excited as I did at sixteen standing in front of the justice of the peace when Larry and I married.

My family and friends are still in shock and can't believe that I accepted "white Dwight's" proposal for marriage. Yes, that's the name they have affectionately called him over the years. I can't believe that I've finally found love and happiness, after so many years of giving up. I still don't know how this white man crept into my life. All that I do know is that my spirit has been replenished.

Ladies, I'm flying high! From sixteen to sixty! Wow! How you like me now?

Chapter Eight

Catherine
Age: 45 - New York, NY

Leesha, it seems that you've managed to triumph over odds that completely overwhelm too many women and you've found a man who sincerely loves you and completely accepts you for who you are. I can only hope that my story has such a happy ending.

My predicament began five months ago and continues to this day. This may sound odd to you but five months ago, on a beautiful Sunday morning, Michael—my husband and the father of our three children, Patrice, 11, Monica, 8, and Michael, Jr., 6—informed me that he was moving to the top floor of our brownstone, and that it was over between us. I was in a state of shock. I had no idea that was coming. At the time, we had been trying to rent that unit for almost six months. I wish now that we had.

Michael had done the same thing three years ago, and said he would never do it again. He realized how badly it affected our children—although they were much younger then—and vowed he would never put them through that again. That's why I was taken off guard.

Ife

True, we continued to have marital problems, but I thought we were dealing with them. The fact is, I hadn't always been faithful, but I thought that Michael and I had gotten past that. I have really hurt Michael—more than once. But that's a part of my past.

Being in a predominately male profession—chemical engineering—I have had a roving eye from time to time. But to be honest, that's not the primary reason we have had problems. Many of the challenges Michael and I face are certainly more than five months old and are based on something that happened to me in my childhood—something that we had been trying to work on together, or so I thought. That's why I'm still not completely sure why he suddenly moved upstairs. He's refused to talk to me about it. Our children, of course, want to know why Daddy isn't sleeping in his bed anymore. I've told them that he has a lot on his mind and needs to be by himself to think, but they're very bright, and I don't think they're buying it. They definitely sense something is wrong. He's a psychologist who works with children; you'd think he'd be a little more sensitive.

I met Michael at New York University while he was in graduate school working on his Masters in psychology. I was there working on my Ph.D. in chemistry. While walking across campus, I heard someone singing. I thought to myself, what a beautiful voice. I turned to see where it was coming from and, to my surprise, saw that this fine man was singing to me. Flattered and embarrassed at the same time, Michael could see how self-conscious I felt and immediately apologized. I assured him that it was all right. It was as though from the moment we spoke, we immediately felt very comfortable with each other. Michael was so handsome, and had such a great personaility. Such a gentleman. Such a voice. And such timing. I met him during one of the lowest points in my life. I had recently returned to campus after an extended leave following my father's death. My father had been sick for a long time when he took a turn for the worst. That was the first year into my doctorate program. I was inundated with work, so I didn't go home to see him when I got the news. Dad had been ill for many years, and over the years, had taken turns for the worst several times. Each time I had gone home to see him. I just thought he would be all right again this time. I was wrong—he died. For a long time I couldn't forgive myself for not saying good-bye. After his funeral, I couldn't sleep, eat, or function. I took time off from school to get myself together. I stayed home with my sister in Springfield, Massachusetts for a couple of months. It took that long to get my head together.

When I returned to the university, I still wasn't myself and continued to feel depressed and guilty about Dad's death. I eventually sought help from a university psychiatrist, Dr. Moreland. He prescribed medication to help me relax and sleep and suggested that I come to see him on a regular basis. I did so for about six months. He really helped me.

But seeing him brought back memories of the last time I had seen a psychiatrist, memories that were still very disturbing for me. I'd started seeing a psychiatrist shortly after my twelfth birthday. That was when I broke down and told my mother that Uncle Bob, her brother, had sexually molested me on several occasions. On occasion Mom would run down to the corner store and leave me with Uncle Bob. Before she could barely close the door, he would look out of the window to make sure she was gone. Then he would start kissing me on my lips and force me to touch him in an inappropriate manner. He would fondle my breasts and grab my butt. He said if I told Mom or Dad, he would do something very bad to me and them. He made me feel so dirty. Keeping that secret ate at my insides. I was confused and angry and never connected my sudden moodiness to the abuse.

Ife

I finally got the courage and told Mom. I was scared, but then so grateful that she believed me without hestation. Mom had already sensed that something was wrong because I had stopped being the happy-go-lucky, talkative little girl she was accustomed to. She had questioned me a couple of times trying to find out what was wrong, but I never revealed this embarassing secret. I eventually became so depressed that I decided if she asked again, I was ready to tell her. So when she asked, I poured my heart out to her. She wanted to know why I hadn't told her. I admitted that I was afraid to tell her or anyone else because Uncle Bob had threatened me, and the family, and had told me that nobody would believe me anyway. I had never before, in all my life, seen Mom so mad. She immediately confronted Uncle Bob. Of course, he denied everything—but Mom didn't believe him. She let him know that he was never to step foot in our house again and that she was going to file a police report. I really don't know what happened to him; I only know I never saw him again. I don't think Mom ever told Dad because she knew he would have killed Uncle Bob. Now that I think about it, maybe she did tell him.

"I sho hopes she did!" says Hattie Mae, who had seemed to be napping.

"Me too. My daddy wouldn't play that stuff, either!" Ena proclaimed.

Ama interrupts several others making similar comments. "OK, ladies, let's allow Miss Catherine to continue. Miss Catherine, go ahead."

Thanks, Ama. Although I saw a psychiatrist for two years after that horrible phase of my life, I don't think that issue has been fully resolved yet. I'm still working on it, as well as several others, with Dr. Moreland's help. You see, I have suffered with depression for a long time, but Dr. Moreland was the first psychiatrist to suggest that maybe my intermittent bouts with depression were related to a chemical imbalance in my brain. He told me if that was the case, there were medications that could correct the condition to the point of reducing the reoccurrence of episodes, or possibly preventing them altogether. He ordered several tests for me and, thank goodness, the results confirmed his theory. I don't want to mislead any of you into thinking I'm fully recovered. I suffer less today, but I've accepted the fact that depression is a serious and sometimes life-long problem.

But now back to Michael. The same day we met, he invited me to dinner. I was hesitant, but I accepted. We had such a good time. It felt as if I had known him for years. That evening, we only spent a couple of hours together because both of us had plenty of work to do. Our schedules were very heavy and neither of us did too much socializing. We were pleased to learn that each of us would complete our degree programs at the end of the semester.

After that first date, Michael and I began to see each other at least once a week. The rest of our story is history. We received our degrees in the May after we met and then decided to stay in New York for a while. Michael and I continued to date, and grew closer and closer, and eventually determined that we were true soul mates.

I began applying for jobs about six months prior to receiving my Ph.D. and had several offers after graduation. My resumé really looked good because I had worked in a chemical lab, part time, for four years prior to receiving my doctorate. I also graduated with honors. I accepted a wonderful job at a major chemical company, with a staggering salary, as lead chemist beading one of the company's highly visible projects. It was a very challenging job. I didn't have a clue that my employment at Keane Laboratories would eventually tear me down—surprisingly, more than my problems with Michael did. Michael wasn't as fortunate in getting the job he really wanted. He accepted a job with the state—counseling run-away kids. The pay was pretty decent, but not what he expected. That was very disappointing to him. I told him not to worry and to look at that job as a stepping-stone to bigger and better things. He always seemed so thankful for my encouragement. I don't think he got too much support in the past. By this time, we were seeing each other every day and soon decided to move in together. That was an extremely happy time for both of us.

To our surprise, after working six months, both of us really liked our jobs. Michael really enjoyed playing a positive role in the lives of the children he counseled. Several kids called often and would come by our apartment to just talk. We loved their company and made each of those visits some kind of learning experience for them. The kids really looked up to Michael, and were so appreciative for the time he spent with them. That made him feel so good.

On my job, I became known for my impeccable work and my ability to work well with everybody. As a result, I was given more to do, as busy employees often are. I was also made the manager of five junior, but experienced, chemists. The more I accomplished, the more they expected of me, and the later I got home every evening. Unfortunately, this interfered with the time I could spend with Michael. He was not too thrilled about my extended hours, but said he understood.

After living together for a little over a year, Michael and I decided to get married. We didn't want a big wedding, because I didn't want my mother to have to bear the expense of it, and I knew she would have insisted. We had a marriage ceremony, officiated by a New York City Justice of the Peace. We invited only my mother, my sister, Michael's grandmother, parents, and brother to the ceremony. His grandmother, who raised him, seemed very happy for him. It was a beautiful celebration!

Eleven months after Michael and I were married, Patrice was born. She was such a gorgeous baby. We hadn't planned on having a baby for a couple of years, and were surprised when I got pregnant so soon. We had no idea what parenting was really about and were a little afraid in the beginning. Courses on parenting were not nearly as popular as they are today, so, naturally, we didn't think to inquire about any. We learned by trial-and-error and, I must say, we have done a commendable job. We have three well-mannered, beautiful children. I really hope our family can remain intact.

About a year after the birth of Patrice, racism reared its ugly head at work. Two of my subordinates, older white men, could no longer *"tolerate"* taking direction from, and being evaluated by me—a younger Black woman—especially in a "man's" profession. I sometimes wonder had I been a light-skinned Black woman with long straight hair, instead of a dark-skinned woman with short natural hair, if I would have been treated the same way—on the job and in other situations as well. But anyway, back to the story. I had sensed their resentment for some time, but never let it interfere with my productivity. Since they were classified as junior chemists when I became their supervisor, they worked very well with me. Once they began to feel confident in their positions, they began to show their true feelings. Despite all the assistance I had given them on many assignments, they began to do things to undermine me. In our weekly meetings, they made disparaging remarks about the way the project was being managed. Although I was upset, angry, and hurt, I was sure that the situation would be resolved quickly and in a professional manner. Boy, was I wrong!

When my immediate supervisor—also a white male—did not support me as I thought he would, and should, I began to feel a great deal of stress. Although I continued to be an excellent performer and function at a very high level, I became melancholy. That feeling was my first conscious sign that something was wrong. I say conscious because other incidents in the past had made me feel the same way, but I hadn't related them to what was going on in my life at the time.

About two years after the problem started, those two guys left the company. But during the height of my employment at Keane Laboratories, I became pregnant with Monica. The timing couldn't have been worse. The pregnancy added another layer of stress to my life, but Michael and I were happy about becoming parents for the second time. We had a lengthy conversation about my pregnancy and whether or not I should continue to work—although in reality we didn't have a choice. Both of us wished that my state-of-mind could have been better. I consciously tried to stay in touch with my feelings and to make sure I handled my daily tasks, at work and at home, in the most positive way possible. I knew that my emotional health, and that of our unborn baby, depended on me taking good care of myself.

At that same time Michael was also beginning to have problems on his job. As odd as it may seem, Michael and I seemed to grow a little closer during that time. We had something in common. Too bad it was something unpleasant, but I believe everything happens for a reason. Michael hadn't received a pay increase since he began his job with the state two years ago. At first, that was okay because he knew how unpredictable state funding could be. For two years, his program didn't receive the funding that was expected. In the third year, funding was reinstated and several of his co-workers received raises, but Michael did not. When he approached his supervisor and was given a really flimsy reason for not receiving a raise, he retreated instead of standing up for himself. I thought he should have been stronger. On several occasions during our marriage, Michael has shown what seemed—at least to me—to be varying degrees of feelings of inadequacy. Sometimes he just didn't seem to have it in him to fight for himself. This was one of those times. We had talked about it before, and during our conversation—more often than not—we concluded that his feelings stemmed from unresolved childhood issues, similar to mine.

Michael and his brother were raised by their grandmother. She was very strict and didn't believe in making a "big-to-do" over their accomplishments. Although Michael's brother didn't seem to care, her attitude really hurt Michael, especially when he was praised by many outside of the family for making the honor roll or being chosen as the main character in school musicals. His beautiful voice always prevailed. But his perception that his grandmother was uncaring still affects him today.

I encouraged Michael to go to his boss and stand up for what was rightfully his. When he finally did, he got a nice pay increase. In the meantime, I was given even more to do on my job. When another lead chemist left for another project, some of his responsibilities were assigned to me, and I was already swamped. The added pressure caused my performance to begin to decline. I had become depressed and my nerves were shot. This was my first real bout with depression since my father died. As the quality of my work declined, I really became agitated and decided to take a short break from the job. I took a week off during a time when I really needed to be at work. However, my mental well-being was much more important than any job. I began seeing Dr. Moreland again at that time. The pressure had reached a point that I became concerned about my overall welfare. Dr. Moreland's counseling and a new medication got me back on track

When I went back to work, I could feel hostility in the air. I just ignored it. I felt one hundred percent better and dove into my work. I was back, and in full force.

During that time, I thought Michael could use a little counseling himself. Around that time Michael, Jr. was also born. Michael and I were fortunate enough to afford to purchase a lovely brownstone and move from our apartment. We desperately needed more space. The girls and I were very happy to have a little boy in the house. He was such a cute and lively baby.

Although Michael was thrilled to have the son he had always wanted, he began to express how inadequate he felt as a father. Michael didn't think he was providing for our children the way he should and that I carried too much of the financial weight. Through the years, his income has never been as much as mine. It was not until he expressed his concern that I knew this was something that bothered him. I assured him I didn't have a problem with our situation and let him know that a partnership is all about working together—each giving one hundred percent. He seemed okay with that, but I guess he really wasn't. Although he's making more money now, I wonder if his surprise move upstairs has anything to do with his insecurity about our financial situation. I guess Michael has quietly been dealing with a lot of stuff for a long time.

After we moved into the brownstone, I began to have more bouts with depression. Although Michael had graciously supported me through all of them, he thought I should take more charge of my life. He may have been right. He told me he had noticed that prior to each episode, I hadn't had my prescriptions refilled. He told me he thought not getting refills was intentional and that maybe I caused these episodes to escape the pressures of life for a little while. I was furious with him for making such an allegation. I had never equated not getting the refills with what was happening to me at the time, but I guess it could have been an unconscious decision. I really don't know.

When I was depressed, Michael literally had to do everything, which, when you have three children can be overwhelming. I think he was growing weary of the burden and hoped my episodes would decrease by now, not increase. With each bout of depression, a little more of the intimacy in our relationship evaporated. This has made me feel guilty and unhappy. I'm sure that this contributed to Michael's decision to move upstairs.

A welcome change occurred in our lives a year and a half ago when both Michael and I got new jobs. My job situation had become unbearable for me. I was literally being worked like a slave. Well, maybe not literally, but it was bad. I finally decided enough was enough and found another challenging position that isn't stressful at all. I no longer supervise anyone and am responsible for my work only. I can work at my own pace. As long as I meet my deadlines, everyone is happy. I haven't missed one yet.

Michael is now with a private firm. He is the director of a program that helps teens cope with everyday issues, many that didn't even exist when we were teens—HIV/AIDS, drive-by shootings, and gang wars, just to mention a few. He also received a sizeable salary increase and seems content with it. I think getting this job boosted his ego tremendously. I'm happy for him.

Still, it has been five months now, and Michael is still upstairs, but finally we have talked about the situation and have mutually agreed to see what happens during the next few months. I have not let the situation stress me out; neither has Michael. I think seeing a psychiatrist for so long has helped me learn to cope with anything I may face—plus Michael and I are not pressuring each other at all. Our primary focus is on the well-being of our three beautiful children. Although the future really doesn't look promising for us, our children are happy. Michael and I made the decision not to let our problems interfere with their well-being. We have continued to do things as a family, including going to church each Sunday. I am hoping that we can bring closure to our situation soon—one way or another.

Despite the things in my life that have led to my bouts of depression—including the chemical imbalance—I'm feeling more comfortable with myself than I ever have been before. I still have a long way to go before I'm completely comfortable with where I am—emtionally, physically and spiritually. That may never happen, but that's all right, too. As long as I am aware of what's really going on with me, I will be alright. I continue to see Dr. Moreland and take my medication, something I may have to do for the rest of my life. I live one day at a time and have decided that since there are no guarantees in life, I'm going to enjoy every minute of every day.

My *spirit* has been on travel for a long time. It's now resting peacefully at home.

Chapter Nine

Makeba
Age: 28 - Los Angeles, CA

I think it's wonderful, Miss Catherine, that you've been able to find a place of equilibrium—not only in your relationship with your husband—but also within your soul. And it's also interesting to me that you wonder whether your dark skin and hair texture have played a detrimental part in how you have been treated. It's interesting because I know for a fact that my light skin, hair, and eyes have been a detriment to me. Had it not been for Jemonte, I might never have discovered that the roots of my soul's equilibrium were in the roots of my own nappy, auburn hair.

With that I will say, "Jambo, all." "Jambo" means hello in Kiswahili. My name is pronounced "Ma-kay-ba." My mother was heavy into South African music when I was born. So that's how I got my name. My story is very different from the others you've heard here. Mine begins with one of my most cherished memories—two short hours that rocked, then changed my world—a two-hour lecture given by Lamin Ture. It was the first time in my adult life, and I'm now 28, that

Ife

I have been so impressed with any single event. Brother Ture's knowledge, the clarity of his reasoning, and his obvious conviction in his beliefs, his confidence in the people to liberate themselves, were astounding, mind altering stuff—at least for me. My boyfriend, Jemonte, practically insisted that I attend the lecture with him. I agreed to go along, but told him not to expect me to get involved. I think he knew what would happen once I heard Brother Ture speak. He thinks he's so slick.

Jemonte, the love of my life, is really quite a guy. Not only is he very intelligent, he's also handsome, dread locks and all. Jemonte is also beautifully Black. He grew up in Compton, the heart of LA's ghetto, but was one of the lucky kids. He lived with both of his parents and attended an independent Black school from the time he was in preschool through graduation from high school. Jemonte always sounds so proud whenever he tells anyone about Umoja Shule, the school, and Baba Imari, the director.

He told me that growing up in the ghetto gave him the opportunity to witness, first-hand, the injustices that have plagued our people for decades—unequal treatment in the "justice" system, including police brutality, institutionalized poverty, and inadequate health care. Even more blatant, he said, were attempts by "the man" to camouflage some of the rip-offs as opportunities for "the disadvantaged" to get goods and services equivalent to those of the "more advantaged." Ha! Jemonte's got what he calls his "rogues gallery of rip-offs"—the schemes that he remembers the most. The landlord tenant thing—for example, landlords collected guaranteed rental payments through government programs, removing their risk of non-payment and getting an excellent income, but still didn't keep the buildings in good repair and cut every corner they could to save a dollar even if it endangered the residents' safety. Another example is the credit-at–the-corner grocery store thing—"Mom and Pop" store owners ran a weekly food-buying tab for selected folk in the neighborhood, then charged them a hefty fee for the privilege.

"I remember that happening in my neighborhood way back when," Marlana comments. "The list goes on and on," she continues.

As a child, Jemonte listened to his mother's brother, Uncle Joe, who had his own stories to tell of the wrongs done to our people. One particular story had a powerful effect on Jemonte; I've heard him tell it several times. Back in the sixties, during a major civil rights demonstration, his Uncle Joe was brutally beaten by the "pigs" (as Uncle Joe still calls them) and arrested for his obvious leadership during the demonstration. Jemonte never forgot this story. That particular incident is one of the primary reasons he works and studies so hard to acquire the skills necessary to help liberate our people. That story, combined with all the others, convinced him that his life's work would be dedicated to making life better for our people in some way. In fact, he believes that all Black people should make some meaningful contribution to the betterment of all our people in honor of our ancestors. Like Lamin Ture, Jemonte understands that Black people must be organized if we are to be liberated. He also believes that the first step toward liberation is study. My exposure to these ideas, through study, has caused me to feel the same way.

Jemonte talked with me many times about joining the National Political Study Program before I decided to go hear Brother Ture's speech. His interaction with the brothers and sisters in the program, and his growing knowledge of the history of our people, seem to keep him on a natural high all the time. He is such a positive brother. That's what attracted me to him in the first place. I really don't know why he was attracted to me, but I think it was because he saw that I was searching at the time—for what, I was not quite sure. Maybe he knew, when I didn't.

My dad retired from the Air Force about nine years ago after twenty-four years of service. He'd been in the Air Force five years when I was born. I am the third child born to my parents. I have an older brother and sister.

Both my dad and mom are very light-skinned. My mom almost looks white. I'm not far from that myself. On top of that I have auburn hair and hazel eyes. But, Hallelujah, I do have beautiful full lips. Got them honestly, from my daddy. Thank goodness that I have at least one prominent African feature!

Dad was an enlisted man who moved through the ranks at a fast pace. He was, and still is, a "true blue" American. He believes in this country and all it supposedly stands for; so does my mom. Dad enjoyed every minute of his active duty. He and Mom both say that they wouldn't be where they are today without the benefit of Dad's being a career military man. They're convinced they would never have gotten the opportunity to travel the world if it had not been for Uncle Sam. They strongly feel that the travel provided additional educational value for my sister, brother, and me, although they weren't thrilled about the constant interruptions in our schooling, moving from one place to another. They are still happily reaping some of the rewards, through veteran's benefits. They definitely deserve them after all the crap Dad, and Mom, and I, for that matter, had to put up with.

Dad wasn't oblivious to the racism and other disheartening conditions that affected Black GI's while he was in the service. He told us stories about being denied certain housing opportunities in some of the locations where he was stationed; and about the ongoing disharmony between the Black and white GI's. His recollections of unfair treatment of Black GI's by white officers, still angers him today.

I'm not as enthusiastic about Dad's military time as he and Mom are. While I admit I enjoyed most of the places where my Dad was assigned, I could have done without the frequent moves. I hated moving from one place to another all the time. It always seemed that as soon as we got settled in a new home and school, it was time to move again. My sister hated moving as much as I did. My brother didn't seem to care one way or the other. I thought it was because boys were just more adventurous. Wasn't that a chauvinistic thought? I have very bad memories of the isolation I felt as a result of not being accepted by the other kids—for being new, for not being Black enough, or white enough, or for being fat. I've always been a little on the plump side, so I got hassled about that as well; I was often called fat and worse by those military kids. I still remember the hurt and pain those names caused me. There were many days when I cried for hours in my room.

Military life left me unable to fit in, feeling invisible at times. I spent much of my childhood wanting to run-away and hide, just disappear. I think the impact of how I was treated by the other kids causes some of my stand-offishness today. Sometimes I still have trouble connecting in social settings. The Black kids didn't particularly like me because they felt as though I thought I was special because I was light-skinned and white kids liked me better than them. But the white kids liked me until they found out I was Black, then they avoided me as well. That went on the entire time Dad was in the military. My brother and sister are both darker than me, more like Dad, so there was never any question about their race; they never seemed to have the problems that I did.

Ife

Thinking back, I now know that my whole life could have been completely ruined because of how my color was perceived. From time to time, my mother would detect my sadness and ask what was wrong. I'd always make up something. I didn't want to tell her what was bothering me for fear that she would think I was being too sensitive and self-conscious about the way I look. Thank goodness for my family's love for me. I believe my secure family life saved me from a whole lot of grief.

Although my interaction with others got a little better by the time I turned eighteen, my day-to-day experiences often made me feel alone. Until I met Jemonte, I had never told anyone the impact military life had on me. In retrospect, I realize I had a crack in my soul. The vision Jemonte has, and Lamin Ture's lecture are the cement that's beginning to mend it. Since that lecture, the repair has escalated. Don't get me wrong, I'm still searching for "my calling." That's one reason Brother Ture's lecture was so important to me, so on target. Jemonte will never fully realize what he has done for me.

I've had a negative self-image for so long, looking white and being Black, being overweight and being treated like fat people are often treated—very mean. From time to time, I wondered had I grown up outside the military, would I have been treated any differently? I guess that's a possibility, but, maybe not. I do know that once Dad retired from the military, the way I was perceived in some environments changed, particularly at Miss Maybelle's place.

Since I was a little girl, I'd always liked doing people's hair. My mother and sister were my on-going guinea pigs. They let me be as creative as I wanted to be styling their hair. As I got older, Mom's friends let me do their hair, too. All that practice, along with my schooling, helped me to become the stylist I am today. As soon as Dad retired, we moved into a Black middle-class neighborhood in Los Angeles, and I started working right away. I was fortunate enough to find rental space to do hair at a combination beauty and barber shop in another Black neighborhood that was not as upscale as the one we lived in. Miss Maybelle owned and ran the shop. From the beginning, I did well and began to build up a clientele. However, as good as I am, one day Miss Maybelle said to me, "Girl, if you want to stay at my shop, you've got to get a license. I don't allow anyone to stay here without one." It took me four months to get my license.

When I started working at the shop, several of the guys that came to get their haircut asked me for a date. That was a real surprise to me because when I was in the military environment, I very seldom got asked out, for all the reasons I've already told you about. So I was apprehensive but glad to finally be asked. I went out with a couple of the barbershop crew. While working there, though, I started putting on a little more weight. Immediately, they stopped showing interest in me. I later learned—through the gossip mill—that those creeps were intrigued with my light skin, auburn hair, and hazel eyes, and that was the main reason the guys wanted to date me. Pitiful, but real! That truth made me so damn mad. I thought, "Here goes this skin color thing again; will it ever go away?" I know the color won't, but I certainly hope the attitudes about my color will.

It was so refreshing to meet Jemonte! From the moment I saw him, I thought he was the truth, and I was right. It was at an African Liberation Day rally downtown. I went strictly out of curiosity. A couple of my clients talked about the great speakers that would be there. They mentioned a few whose names I was familiar with, but I'd never heard them speak. I am ashamed to say it now, but I really wasn't that knowledgeable about the history of our people.

Ife

Jemonte was definitely into the entire aura of the rally. He was wearing a beautiful dashiki, his dreads were neatly styled in an unusual way and looked real cool. You know I paid special attention to his head—the hair dresser in me, I guess. He was listening intently to every speaker and gave the Black power sign whenever he agreed with what they said—which was a lot. I stood right next to him, so when I subconsciously responded in a negative way to something one of the speakers said, Jemonte heard me and said, "My sister, what's your disagreement with what the sister said?" That's where it all began with Jemonte and me.

I was in awe during my first session at the National Political Study Program. The program involves reading, studying and discussing a book every month, and doing some much needed work in the community. Community projects are chosen by consensus of the combined study groups, and most of them involve a lot of physical labor.

The sessions for the first part of the study program are held every other week. Everyone in each group, and there are several concurrent groups, is required to participate during each session. I sat in on the group Jemonte is in, but was told if I became an active participant, I would be assigned to another group. I wondered why.

An awesome list of questions is developed for every study session, and each answer requires such a high level of thought. A group coordinator is responsible for soliciting answers from all participants. Those who don't come prepared to discuss the assigned material are harshly criticized by the group. It is made very clear that the Program is about much more than reading; it's about studying, organizing, understanding, and doing. Although I was there only as an observer at my first session, I felt quite intimidated by what I saw.

Cancer *of the* Spirit

Jemonte told me that many of the sisters and brothers in the study groups have either finished college or taken a few courses. Since I've taken no college courses at all, once again I began wondering if I would, or even could, fit in. A feeling of unadulterated fear came over me, but I dealt with it.

I've been participating in the National Political Study Program for six months now and have found that I can hang. I was assigned to one of the smaller study groups, three sisters and three brothers. This increased my fear because I knew I would have to participate more. But I'm reading, learning and participating; and I can't believe how my world view is changing and expanding. Having been brought up in a military environment, and raised by parents who bought into the "land of the free and home of brave" hype, and passed it on to me, had blinded me to so many truths. I'm not blaming my parents, or anyone else for that matter, for not telling me the truth, or not even really knowing what it is. It's not as though the information is readily available; you have to search it out. My family would definitely benefit from the study program. That's a nice thought—them attending and all—but I know that will never happen in this life. They are too deep into and too consumed by, what they think of as the "good life."

The book assigned the first month I attended the study group was *"How Europe Underdeveloped Africa,"* by Walter Rodney. Have any of you ever read it? I tell you it was an eye-opener for me! I was fortunate enough to have Jemonte to pre-discuss the book with me. And he didn't cut me any slack in the discussions we had, either. I got a little angry at him a couple of times, even though I knew he was helping to prepare me for the study group. I also now understand why the program does not allow girlfriends and boyfriends, husbands and wives, or others in close relationships to be in the same study group. The dis-

Ife

cussions can get real heated as ideas and perceptions and misconceptions are addressed. It's all good, though.

Walter Rodney's book took me back to Lamin Ture's lecture, where many untruths about the history of our people were revealed to me. Before that I simply had no clue as to how much I didn't know. It's made me wonder about all the lies our people have been told, and are still being told. I became fully committed to the Program after reading that book. I knew somehow that my finding out more about my people's history would help me learn more about myself, including my fear of not fitting in and my ambivalent feelings about my skin color.

I have finally internalized that although I look the way I do, I am a descendant of Africans and, therefore, am an African myself. I derive a great sense of pride from this knowledge. And, because I now have a better understanding of my people's proud history, I am becoming more and more content with who I am. I, like all other Africans here, just happened to be born in this country. When I discuss this with my sister, brother, and parents, they think I've lost my mind. Although they're very proud to be Black, they have a problem being referred to as Africans. I hope they get it one day.

By sharing this new-found love of knowledge, Jemonte and I have grown so much closer. He is so proud of my political development. I must say that I am proud of me, too, and feeling so much better about myself. I have developed a special bond with the members of the group. From day one, they looked past my color and my weight, and accepted me for who I am. I did have some concerns about how I would be viewed in such a group, especially after Jemonte told me that the way I look even had an impact on him when we first met. It wasn't a positive impact either. He is so Afro-centric. He really had reservations about dealing with me at first. He finally came to the conclusion that he wasn't that shallow, and that I am just as African as he is— just another shade in the rainbow of African hues. I'm struggling mentally and physically to overcome this weight thing. I've learned through the study group that it's just as important to be physically fit as it is to be mentally fit. My comrades have informed me, although it's unbelievable to me, that the physical labor for the program is sometimes much harder than the mental labor. So much work needs to be done in the Black community, both physical and mental. Considering what lies ahead of me, being forty pounds overweight is no joke. To prepare myself, I started doing high-impact aerobics four weeks ago— one hour sessions, three times a week. I go to the gym and I follow a plan that not only allows me to workout but also offers sessions on how to eat properly and realistically monitor my weight. So far it's working! Another reason that I care for Jemonte so much is because he has never said anything negative about my weight. He has constantly told me what a beautiful queen I am, even when I had doubts myself. I sometimes still do, but I am slowly overcoming that too, especially now that I see a few pounds disappearing. I'm so very happy with my life!

Always for the people!

Chapter Ten

Sharon
Age: 55 - Bowie, MD

My life, like most others, has presented challenges, disappointments, and heartache. Each in its turn has come and, when its time was up, has gone. Knowing always that pain ends and all problems can be resolved has been my saving grace from as early as I can remember. As a result, I can honestly say my life has been wonderful; that is not to say "perfect"—for perfection leaves no room for growth or enlightenment. Yes, my life has been wonderful because every phase of it has brought me a special kind of joy, although I may not have realized it at the time.

I was born on January 6th. That places me under the astrological sign of Capricorn—the goat. "Stubborn as a goat" is a description that fits me perfectly. My parents, Emmanuel and Daisey Sampson, had three girls, Arlene, Louise, and me. I'm the oldest. My family moved from Knoxville, Tennessee to Brevard, North Carolina when I was just two years old. That's where my father's mother, Grandmom, lived. We went to North Carolina with the hope that my dad would find work that was more challenging and paid more. Mom, Arlene, Louise, and I didn't stay in Brevard too long, though—only until I finished first grade. Mom left Daddy and moved us to Camden, New Jersey because Daddy had a terrible drinking problem and he had no interest in getting rid of it. Mom also had a brother, Uncle Greg, who lived in Camden. When I was ten, an aunt told me that Mom had threatened to leave Daddy a year or so before she did, but gave him a chance to change his ways. When he didn't, she left. We weren't in Camden six months before Daddy showed up and convinced Mom to take him back. He stopped drinking for a while, but that didn't last long. In fact, his drinking got worse as we got older. As a kid, I wondered why Mom put up with Daddy's foolishness. He was a totally different person when he was drinking.

When we were little, the neighborhood kids loved Daddy because often on Saturdays, and usually after he'd had a few drinks, he would do magic shows, tap dance, sing, or do some other fun things with us. We really enjoyed those times with him. Frequently, as a show of affection, Daddy would grab Mom and us and rub our cheeks with his whiskers. That always made us laugh, but aggravated us at the same time. When he wasn't drinking, you wouldn't have known that he was the same man. He was so laid back and hardly said a word. Another thing he did while "under the influence," was use foul language. Daddy never did anything to harm us, but had a "cussing" vocabulary that you wouldn't believe! He used that awful vocabulary to "protect" us. He "cussed out" young and old guys in our neighborhood for no other reason than they paid attention to "his girls." Daddy sure knew how to embarrass us.

Ife

Daddy finally stopped drinking about twelve years before he died—at the age of eighty. His incentive came from a county judge who threatened to "lock him up" if Mom reported his drunken behavior again. During those sober years Daddy tried to help several of the younger alcoholics in the neighborhood turn their lives around. Surprisingly, they listened to him because they remembered him "when"—when he drank as much or more than them. We were so proud when he stopped drinking.

Mom and Daddy were so different. To this day, I've never seen her take even a sip of alcohol. She never smoked either. Daddy did a whole lot of both. Mom was a regular churchgoer; she sang in the choir and taught Sunday school and Bible classes. She raised my sisters and me to be active church members, too. Daddy was not a churchgoer at all. I sometimes wondered how they got together. For obvious reasons, I'm happy that they did.

Being raised by an alcoholic, but hard working, father and a mother who had to struggle to make ends meet, made me feel insecure and unsure about what was going to happen next. That uncertainty carried over into my adult life for a long time and made me question almost everything—Am I doing this right? Am I doing that right? Am I doing a good job as a mother, wife, daughter, sister, aunt, employee?—and on and on.

Growing up in Camden was relatively uneventful. My family lived in a section called Third Ward. It was one of Camden's working class neighborhoods. Most of the families in our neighborhood owned their own homes. Although not expensive, they were modest homes that everyone kept up—except Uncle Greg. We lived in a house that my mother's brother, Uncle Greg, owned. There were often things in the house that needed repair. Many times major repairs weren't taken care of in a timely manner. I think Uncle Greg felt that his "real" tenants, in the other buildings he owned, should be taken care of first. After all, we were only family, and probably paid less rent, if any at all.

I enjoyed my elementary, junior high, and high school days so much that I always tried to do my best and had perfect attendance except for a couple of years. I was disappointed, though, that I didn't get to attend the high school of my choice. The dividing line for both high schools went right up the middle of our street. Kids on one side of the street went to Woodrow Wilson High, and the other kids went to Camden High. Woodrow Wilson had predominately Jewish students at the time, while Camden High was what we would today call highly diversified. I lived on the Woodrow Wilson side of the street. With the exception of one girlfriend, all of my friends went to Camden High. Even though I missed my friends terribly, I enjoyed high school. And after graduating, I was off to Howard University in Washington, D.C.—which was at first, a shock since I hadn't even applied to Howard.

I had spent the previous year convincing one of my best girlfriends, Laura, to attend college with me at North Carolina College, where I had applied. I had already been accepted, and when she was accepted, we were elated. It was not hard to convince her to apply to NCC. My sisters and I, and most of our first cousins, spent all or part of every summer in Brevard, North Carolina. Laura had gone with us the previous summer, and we had met several handsome young men there who attended NCC.

So when my mother told me that I was going to Howard, I was shocked, to say the least. She had applied to Howard for me and informed me of her decision only three days before I was to leave for North Carolina College. Needless to say, I was very disappointed. Laura went to NCC anyway, but only stayed one semester. To this day, I feel a little guilty about that situation.

My mother then had another surprise for me. She informed me that I would be staying with her sister, Aunt Roslyn, who lived in Washington, DC, rather than living on campus. That's when the goat in me really came out. I let my mother know, in no uncertain terms, that I would not do any studying if I couldn't live on campus. Since she knew how bull-headed I was, she consented. Some nerve I had, since I didn't have a dime to pay for anything. Mom and Daddy didn't have much more. They really had to sacrifice to send me to college. Thank goodness I had support from extended family, particularly Aunt Roslyn and a cousin who lived in DC. But it turned out that my mother's decision to send me to Howard was one of the best decisions she ever made regarding my well-being and it created one of the happiest circumstances of my life.

I hadn't been on campus forty-eight hours before I met Anthony (Tony) S. Bradford, Jr. I remembered seeing him the first day, in the cafeteria. Our actual meeting, however, occurred on the second day at the Freshman dance on the parking lot behind the Fine Arts building. It was ironic because he later told me that I was specifically pointed out to him on the first day. He had boasted to a freshman buddy that the girls at Howard weren't as pretty as those at his high school. That buddy said to him, "One of these young ladies is going to knock you right out of your chair, and there she is." That was me. Our time at Howard was one of the best phases of both of our lives. We married during our senior year. We have been together ever since that freshman dance forty-one years ago. Just last March we celebrated our thirty-eighth wedding anniversary. Tony and I still remark on how fortunate we were to meet the right person the first time. Our loving advice to couples today, especially newlyweds, is to "never stop honeymooning!" We haven't, and don't plan to.

Howard University still plays a prominent role in our lives. Tony has been an employee there for the last thirty-one years, and our three wonderful children, two sons and a daughter, have all attended Howard at one time or another.

Our children, Kamari, Ayana, and Addae, all grown now, have been an ongoing joy in our lives. Our oldest son Kamari has been into music since he was eleven years old and organized a neighborhood band—the Funk Invaders. Kamari is a music producer and co-owner of a growing recording studio, K. O. Productionz.

Our daughter, Ayana, finished her undergraduate work at Spelman College in Atlanta and completed dental school at the University of Maryland, then specialized in endodontics (root canals) at the University of Iowa. Her husband, Eddie, a Morehouse grad, also attended the University of Iowa where he recently received a doctorate in pharmacy.

Addae, our youngest son, had been a much loved and highly praised teacher until the charter school where he taught was suddenly closed. Addae now co-owns a moving company. Like Kamari, he is also musically inclined—a rap artist and lyric writer. He works with Kamari and a cousin, who is also a song-writer.

One of the greatest sources of Tony's and my happiness is our grandchildren. For many years, Tony and I wanted grandchildren. Now we have two—really five. Ayana and Eddie's daughter, Ani, is truly a joy to all. Kamari's adorable, very active two-year old son is JJ.

Ife

Our sons' significant others have three children. One has two and the other has one and JJ. Both of my sons are in relationships that have lasted for more than five years. Since Tony and I would like a few more grandchildren, I hope they will be ready for marriage soon, but we understand their desire to "make it" professionally before making a lasting commitment.

Like any other family, we have faced our share of challenges, but we have always worked together to resolve them. This approach has been most effective. Kamari and Addae, for example, have worked very hard—Kamari for over fifteen years—to build their businesses. They have not had the level of success that they expected, but have continued on a steady path to reach their goals. We hope this will be the year that both of them solidly establish themselves financially.

We will continue to support them in their endeavor to become completely independent and self-reliant, as long as they continue to work as hard as they are doing now.

An ongoing challenge that involved Tony, and a couple of stressful issues, arose several years ago. At the time, Tony was Howard University's Dean for Residence Life, responsible for the well-being of the 3,400 students living in the dormitories. The university's administration changed and Tony's boss and mentor retired. At the same time, Tony was also beginning to feel burned out and wanted to change his position at the university. He thought there were other opportunities where he would be able to offer fresh ideas and still continue to be a positive influence on students. The various changes at the university placed him in a somewhat tenuous situation for almost two years.

Tony got through that very trying period with my full support. But by the time the situation became more favorable for him, I realized that

Cancer *of the* Spirit

Tony's anguish had taken its toll on me. Once I *knew* Tony was all right, I was all right, too. At the same time, I was under pressure on my job. I was the Deputy Program Manager of an information systems company. One of my major responsibilities was to direct and work as a member of the marketing team. Our job was to continuously identify and bring new business into the company. In retrospect, I know that Tony's challenges at work, coupled with my own, had a negative effect on me. I didn't realize it, but I was "down in the dumps." I often felt exhausted, and many days wished I didn't have to go to work. But I knew, as I tell myself in any situation of adversity, "This too shall pass."

For seventeen years, I had worked consecutively for four minority-owned management consulting firms, owned by individuals who I had the utmost respect for— two women and two men. Each of those experiences opened my eyes to different realities of the business world. One of the four experiences was a very good one. Two of them taught me some hard lessons about life, and the other one was a most depressing experience. All four allowed me to see how naive I was, particularly about some of the things that go on in the workplace. Thinking back, all of my bosses were pretty complex people, and more than likely, were facing issues of their own.

It is ironic that my most depressing employment situation was at Basic Tech—my next-to-last job. I actually interviewed for the position of Senior Vice President three times before deciding to accept it. I wanted to be sure that the CEO's and my management styles, philosophies, and workplace ethics were compatible. After several meetings, I was convinced that they were. I could not have been more wrong! During the one year I was with the company, I discovered that the CEO was a real fake. She pretended to care so much about the employee's welfare. One by one, they discovered the only person she cared about was herself.

Ife

My first five months with the company were wonderful. Although I was diagnosed with breast cancer during my first month there, she paid me for the time I had to take off to recover from surgery. I will always be grateful for that. I later came to realize, however, that most of the other employees were treated horribly and unfairly. Everyone was treated badly, from top management to clerical staff, unless the CEO liked you personally. That was the sole basis of her discriminatory treatment. Even if you were one of the *"lucky"* ones, you still caught hell every now and then. I had real problems with that and was often told by her that I was "too compassionate." I, like several of the other managers, would leave work each day with knots in my stomach. And it wasn't only employees who were treated badly; contractors were also treated unjustly and often didn't get paid on time. That's how bad it was. The company's major contract was with the federal government—and we all know that you don't "play" with the government.

Over time, differences in management styles, as well as overall business and personal ethics, caused a rift between the CEO and myself that led me to resign. Turns out that resigning when I did was one of the best decisions of my life. Shortly thereafter, the company was shut-down by the government for mismanagement. I, along with several other employees, was called to testify before a Grand Jury. Because of the high-level position I'd held, anything could have happened. That was one of the scariest experiences that I've ever had. Still I imagine it must have been even scarier for the CEO, who I later heard was incarcerated for fraud. My misread of her still amazes me today. I'm usually very good at "reading" people, but I was way off with that one.

As I mentioned, the beginning of my challenges with that job was also the beginning of my most major health challenge. It was at the end of 1992 when I was diagnosed with breast cancer. The evening when Tony and I sat down with Dr. Nealson, we were both so sure the news was going to be positive. When it wasn't, I was taken so off guard, it took me a little time to regroup and ask her what the next step was. I let her know I was ready to take it, whatever it was.

The diagnosis was a complete surprise to me. My annual mammogram hadn't shown a problem. A couple of months after my mammogram, I had a gut feeling that something wasn't right. I guess it was my inner spirit speaking to me. I decided to see a a female doctor referred to me by my gynecologist. That's when I met Dr. Nealson. When she first examined me, she didn't think anything was unusual but wanted to administer another test, just to be sure. I'm so grateful to her. Although Dr. Nealson's news was disturbing and scary, it didn't overpower me, despite the fact that I'd heard so many sad stories about the devastation of breast cancer. It's such a deadly disease. I don't know why I wasn't scared out of my mind, but I'm so glad that I wasn't. I now know that the way I responded to the news, as well as the way I handled myself during those first six weeks after my surgery, had an enormous impact on how everyone around me handled their emotions, especially Tony, Ayana, Kamari, and Addae.

It's been over eleven years since my surgery on December 29, 1992. I am one of the many blessed breast cancer survivors. Early detection was the key to my survival. I'm also fortunate to have an abundance of support from a wonderful family and great friends. The greatest blessing of all was that the cancer had not spread and no follow-up treatment was necessary. The medical care provided by Howard University doctors, nurses, interns, and other staff was outstanding. These and numerous other blessings permitted my morale to remain amazingly high, helping me to get through a potentially very low and depressing period in my life. I made a conscious decision to rise above and survive my health challenge. It hasn't always been easy though!

I firmly believe that one of the major reasons I have had such a positive outlook on my personal experience with breast cancer is because, at a very early age, Mom repeatedly told my sisters and me that, "Pretty is as pretty does." I wish this could be instilled in every baby girl. I think it would have a profound positive impact on them for the rest of their lives.

Many women are totally devastated by having a mastectomy, the "disfiguring" surgery that is often the treatment for breast cancer. Unfortunately, we live in an "image conscious" society, and many women who accept its limitations feel that losing one or both breasts is the end of the world. They literally think that their womanhood has been taken away. I dare not minimize the very real, frightening, and definitely devastating feelings of my fellow breast-cancer survivors. I can whole-heartedly relate to them, but I do believe we should take a step back and examine what's really important in our lives. We should be at the top of our own list. Not our spouse, our children, our family, our friends, our job, or anything else. And certainly not a sexist image mired in outdated beliefs. We should be the most important person to us. Most women have been brought up to think that taking care of themselves first is a selfish way of thinking—but is it really? If we don't care for ourselves first, and now, we won't be able to care for others now or later.

Most of us have been programmed to accept the superficial trappings related to body image that society constantly projects. Many breast cancer survivors have been devastated by the disappearance of a spouse, companion, or male friend along with the "disappearance" of a breast. I say, those guys needed to go. If your breasts were the only part of you they valued, you're better off letting their "shallow asses" go anyway. In the long run, you will be the beneficiary of their absence.

Unfortunately, that isn't the end of my unexpected challenges. A little over seven years ago, I was declared disabled as a result of a condition caused by my breast cancer surgery. I have problems with swelling in my right arm and hand, which really restricts what I can do, especially since I am right-handed. Since then, I have been unable to work. Prior to my disability, I was Director of Business Development for one of the minority-owned firms I previously mentioned. I really enjoyed my job. I was always meeting and interacting with new people. Being a "people person," that position was perfect for me. The other major component of my position, which is a part of the reason I was declared disabled, was proposal writing. I had to work at the computer, writing for hours at a time. As a marketer as well, I had to handle equipment, marketing materials, and other fairly heavy items, used for giving presentations in locations all over the metropolitan area.

My spirit was extremely low the first year and a half I was at home. I had worked for twenty years, and it was very difficult for me to be at home. What made it even more difficult was I couldn't do all the things I was used to doing around the house because most of those activities required constant use of my arms and hands. But I've learned to adjust and do different things now.

Being at home has allowed me the time to simply sit and think about my life and all the challenges I've experienced, all the people who have passed through my life and the impressions they've left

Ife

behind. I think about my father and how glad I am that he and mom found each other. Needless to say, I wouldn't be around if they hadn't. I've thought about my children and the positive contributions they've made to my life and Tony's as well. I've thought about our grand-children and what a true blessing they are. I've reflected, with an abundance of gratitude, on what a remarkable experience I've had after my surgery and subsequent recovery from breast cancer. And finally, I've thought about the joy I've experienced through writing.

Almost five years ago, when the idea for writing a book came to me, I sat down and began to do just that. The discovery that I could write a little each day was awesome. Writing has allowed me to con-nect with my true spirit. Not only is writing compatible with my spir-it, it is also a way that I can connect with many others—especially women—and contribute to the empowerment of womankind. Writing certainly has empowered me. By writing just a page and a half or two pages a day, and not everyday, I've now completed my first book. That has been the most exciting and purposeful venture I have ever under-taken. When it's published, and I am confident that it will be, I'll let all of you know. And just for the record, I've already begun writing my second book, *All Of A Sudden It Was Too Late.*

This has been an awesome gathering, ladies. Thanks again, Ama.

"What's the title of your first book? I can't wait to get a copy," shouts Leesha.

Chapter Eleven

Ama
Age: 32 - Morristown, NJ

I cannot possibly thank you all enough for coming here this weekend, especially knowing what a long trip it was for some of you. I had really hoped by bringing together Ma's best friends and mine, we would create a sort of cross-generational energy, which I could somehow infuse into my program for at-risk youth—and through that, into the lives of the kids I want to help. Some of my kids are abandoned, or living in homes with alcoholic parents; some have been sexually and psychologically abused by caregivers or even their peers; and some of them come from such depressing circumstances that even I don't know how they cope. Your personal stories have given me a better insight about their situations, and how to help. This has turned out to be a weekend Ma would really have enjoyed and cherished. I certainly have—and will.

As most of you already know, I was only ten when Ma first learned she had lung cancer; I was fifteen when she died. I thought Ma's death was the end of my world. Although I now realize that she and Pop did all they could to prepare me for her death, that didn't matter at the time. She was gone, and I was devastated.

You may know, Auntie Marla, that Ma was deeply depressed after her doctor told her that she had cancer. She had stopped smoking about seven years before that. She had decided to be a lot more health-conscious, and smoking was one of her first "bad habits" to go. She was so sad once she got the news. I was very worried about her, and so afraid of what was going to happen to her, and to me and Pop. But once she saw how distressing the news was to me, she tried to comfort me by holding me tightly in her unusually frail, weak arms. She tried to assure me that we were going to get through this thing—and for several years we did.

Almost two years after Ma began her radiation treatments, her cancer went into remission. We all breathed a sigh of relief, especially, Pop, who had a real rough time accepting that she had cancer. I figured it had to be rough on him, yet he didn't seem sensitive or sympathetic enough about Ma's condition. I think he assumed that since she hadn't stopped working, she was all right. Ma needed to keep herself occupied. She kept working because it helped keep her mind occupied with something other than her cancer. She was so tired at the end of each day, but that didn't stop Pop from making the same demands on her that he always had. At times, he even seemed angry about her illness. That made me so mad. Thinking back on it now, and having learned so much since then, I believe that Pop's reaction to Ma's illness was out of absolute fear and a sense of helplessness. He was losing Ma and just didn't know what to do.

At the same time, though, I had a problem coping myself. I continued to go out with my friends and do the things junior high school kids did, some of which were not too positive—like playing hooky, spending way too much time on the phone, and chasing boys when I should have been studying. I suppose I, too, was trying to ignore Ma's cancer by not accepting the possibility that her remission might be temporary. I continued to do some things I knew I shouldn't be doing. I'm not even sure that I realized it at the time. Ma and Pop, particularly Ma, tried to hide the worst of her illness from me, and tried to make every day seem as "normal" as possible under the circumstances.

Ma and Pop always made so many sacrifices for me, so when feelings of guilt would overtake me, I would think, "Ma and Pop have always made sure I never wanted for anything, and this is how I repay them." Once the realization that Ma could really die actually sunk in, I began to think that somehow my actions had aggravated her condition. That revelation began my journey to maturity. For the first time, I realized that all of my actions had consequences and that I had better be willing to live with them—whatever they were—for the rest of my life. That realization was my first step on the path to adulthood. I was fourteen at the time and had so much to learn.

Ma's remission lasted two years. Then the cancer returned with a vengeance. It quickly spread into her chest and finally into her bones. She lived for only one more year.

Ma's last year with Pop and me was tough. There was so much about her situation that I didn't understand. Ma never talked much about the specifics of her illness, and when she was in pain, she tried so hard to hide it. I knew when she ground her teeth she was having a lot of pain. I could also tell by the strained look on her face. She was in pain much more often than we knew. When she stayed at home and in bed for most of the day, we knew for sure because that was so unlike her. Ma was never one to complain about anything. And she was very religious. She believed that through prayer, she would eventually get well. She and Pop raised me in the church, and I was taught to believe in the power of healing through prayer. I remember I prayed with all my heart every day. When Ma continued to get worse, I wondered why my prayers weren't being answered. Ultimately, I wondered what I had done that was so wrong that God would do this to Ma and to me. A remnant of that feeling, despite all that I've learned about faith and about cancer since then, remains with me.

After her courageous five-year battle with cancer, Ma died peacefully in Pop's arms. Both Pop and I were at her bedside when we realized she was slipping away. She told us how tired she was and said she thought she was on her way home soon. She was so calm. Her whisper became a bit louder when she told us how much she loved us and asked us to take good care of each other. I had a hard time staying in the room after that, but somehow I managed. That was the saddest day of my life. Excuse me for a second. I'll be OK.

After Ma's death, Pop was so lost that he didn't realize how lost and lonely I was without her, or how withdrawn I had become. I wanted him to comfort me, like Ma would have if he had been the one who had died. I now know that most men have a harder time giving comfort than receiving it. I think that's primarily because of the different way men and women are raised. Ma had always been there to comfort me. We were so close. Even during my challenging teen years, Ma was a good listener. We didn't always agree, but we had such great conversations. She was so easy to talk to, and always gave me good, reasonable advice. There was nothing that I couldn't tell her.

Cancer of the Spirit

Pop, on the other hand, was not a good listener. Most of the time, he didn't even let me finish what I was saying before he chimed in. He always had to have the last word. Lots of times, Ma had to say, "Now George, listen to your daughter. Give her a chance to finish what she's saying." But he would cut Ma off, too. Both of us found it very difficult to talk to him. I suppose he must have had a lot on his mind. He always seemed so preoccupied.

When Ma died, I had a really hard time accepting it, particularly during the first two months after. I was really hurting and so lonely. I went to school and hung out some with my friends, but I had really begun to withdraw. I spent a lot of time at home alone. It took Pop about six months after Ma's death to realize how much I'd withdrawn. Once he did, he tried hard to assure me that we were going to be fine. The one thing Pop did that helped me more than anything else, was to get me involved in more of the youth activities at our church. I was already involved in Sunday school and the Young People's Choir, but had begun sleeping in on Sundays and missing rehearsals. Since Pop was very active in the church, and always went to choir rehearsals and deacon's board meetings several times a month, he started insisting I go with him. The youth activities were usually going on at the same time.

At first, I didn't want to go—I just had no interest. I preferred spending time with my school friends or just being by myself at home. But Pop insisted that I become more involved with the kids and the activities at church, which he hoped would provide some spiritual uplifting that would help me better understand and accept Ma's death, as well as help me focus on something other than her death. Looking back, I am so glad he insisted, even though I was really "ticked" at the time!

Ife

Once I started going to church, I began to recall the many conversations that Ma, Pop, and I had when we were preparing for her death. Ma's powerful words about prayer and trusting in the Lord came back. Recalling her words, in that atmosphere, made me a little more accepting of her death. Pop was also right about the spiritual boost he thought the kids from church would give me.

Although I had attended church all of my life with Ma and Pop, I hadn't paid any attention to how different the kids at church were from the friends I had at school. At first, I thought they were weird, being so much into the Lord and all. The more I participated in the activities with them, the more I liked going to church, and the more I enjoyed being around them. There was one kid I liked more than the others. His name was Teddy Carpenter.

Teddy was seventeen but he wore corn-rows that made him look younger. He had a contagious smile and beautiful sparkling white teeth. That's what first caught my eye. Ma was such a stickler when it came to oral hygiene. Anyway, Teddy, like me, was a newcomer to the youth group. That gave us something in common and made us feel more comfortable with each other.

I didn't tell Pop about Teddy right away. Any time I had shown interest in a boy, Pop made sure that it didn't go any further than interest. I thought maybe he would act differently about Teddy since he was a church kid but I wasn't sure. Still, I planned to tell him about Teddy before someone else did, but I wasn't quite ready. Besides, Pop was very happy to see how my involvement in church had changed me. We continued to have disagreements about most things, but we got along somewhat better once I became interested in more church activities. But then, about midway through my junior year, Pop began to restrict my association with my school friends. He said they were headed nowhere fast and told me he preferred that I keep my distance. I became very angry, and told him I was old enough to choose my own friends, and all of them didn't have to be kids from our church. My friends, the ones at school and at church, were a haven from my loneliness. They had really helped me cope with the loss of Ma. I became so angry with him for trying to take away the solace I'd found. During a very heated argument, I blurted out my growing interest in Teddy. That certainly was not the way I wanted to break the news to him. Anyway, Pop told me I was being disrespectful. Whether I liked it or not, he expected me to abide by what he said. Furthermore, he wanted to know all about "this Teddy," and insisted that I invite him and his parents to dinner. As it turned out, that was the best thing that could have happened. Seems Pop already knew Teddy's parents. He was on a couple of church committees with them. And, to my astonishment, he really liked Teddy—corn-rows and all!

My senior year at Jackson, however, was another story. It started off touch-and-go. I had just turned seventeen and Pop continued to try to restrict my contact with my friends at school, which only heightened the rebellious streak already brewing. I had done so well in school prior to his restrictions. I deliberately slacked off studying. I had already taken the PSATs during my junior year so I could get a head start in preparing myself for college. My scores were very decent. So I made up my mind not to do my best during my senior year, knowing that would be a way to get back at Pop. And it worked. He was very disappointed with my grades during the first quarter, but he warned me that if I didn't get back on track, I wouldn't be going away to college. As parents often do, he saw right through my plan and beat me at my own game. He knew how much I wanted to go away to college, and

Ife

that I would do whatever it took to make that happen. It goes without saying that I quickly changed my mind about not preparing for the SATs. I had to take the tests at the beginning of the third quarter, so I broke down and asked Pop to buy me the study guide. That request pleased him, and he bought it the same day I asked.

Since I knew the SAT scores would be a major factor in determining what college I could attend, I studied like never before. I wanted to score as high as possible so I could receive several scholarship offers and attend the college or university of my choice. Living at home with Pop while I attended college was *not* an option. Don't get me wrong, I love Pop, but it was very difficult living alone with him. When Ma was alive, I had an ally. But he was so stubborn and opinionated, I thought going away to school would be just as good for Pop as it would be for me.

My second quarter grades improved, but I still hadn't put forth my best effort. During the third and forth quarters, all I did was study. My friends accused me of having tunnel vision and becoming very boring. They reminded me that it was my senior year and I needed to have some fun. To be honest, I wasn't too pressed about celebrating my senior year. I had *thoroughly* enjoyed my freshman, sophomore, and junior years. Between studying for the SATs and my five courses, I didn't have time, nor did I want time, to do anything else. My concentrated effort paid off. I scored 1250 on the SAT, and got all A's and two B's during the third and fourth quarters. Shortly into the fourth quarter, I began receiving acceptances from schools all around the country. I chose Prairie View A&M in Houston, Texas because its sociology department and school of social work had outstanding reputations. Since my long-range goal was to head a program for at-risk youth, Prairie View was an excellent choice. Once I'd made my choice, I really became excited. The thought of leaving home and being on my own was thrilling. Pop seemed a little sad about my leaving, though. He never said so, but I could clearly tell. I knew he wanted me to stay close by, but there was no way that I was going to stay in town.

I had a jamming going-away party to say good-bye to my family, friends, and, of course, Teddy. It was both a happy and sad occasion. The music was slamming and the food was off-the-hook. Everyone there was very happy for me. Knowing that it would be a while before we saw each other again, made things a little melancholy—but only for a minute. I realized how much I missed Ma when the DJ played a song that we used to dance to. Although I knew she was with me in spirit, I wished she could have been there in body as well.

On the morning that I was to leave for Texas, Teddy came by and helped me and Pop load the mini-van. We packed every inch of it. I didn't realize how much stuff I had until we finished packing that van. Because I was going such a long way from home, we thought it would be wise to take as much as I could. Teddy made me promise to keep in touch and said he would try to visit. I definitely planned to keep in close contact with him.

Pop and I left Morristown, New Jersey, that August, headed for Prairie View. I was so excited! Pop decided, instead of rushing, to make the trip in three days. I knew he wanted to spend some quality time with me since he knew I would be gone for a long time—possibly, for good.

My plan was to come back home during the summers to work. It didn't work out that way, though. I loved the program at Prairie View. It was much more interesting than I thought it would be. Several of my instructors were fascinating, and one in particular—Dr. Mahan. Her course, "The Philosophy of Social Work," was very challenging, to say the least. The subject matter was really complex. I can proudly say I enjoyed it more than any other course. I got an A+. Most of my friends at Prairie View, some who were fellow classmates, had very sharp minds. They were real intellectuals. They were from all over the country and were so diverse in their backgrounds and thinking. This made our classes all the more stimulating. I looked forward to going to every class—quite different from my high school days. I thought of Ma often and how proud of me she would be.

Since I didn't go home during the summer, I was allowed to stay in my dorm room. That was really a blessing. I had so much stuff.

My freshman year seemed to fly by. Near the end of it, I found out that Prairie View had a summer work-study program that provided room and board and a small stipend to students fortunate enough to be chosen. Although the program was year-round, freshmen and sophomores could only apply for work during the summer. Since I did so well in my classes all year, I applied for the program just to see what would happen. Being a freshman, I didn't think I had a chance of being chosen. I was shocked when I was selected for the *Listen to Students Program.*

When I told Pop I was going to apply for the program, he encouraged me to do so, but I think he was as shocked as I was when I was selected. He tried to sound happy for me, but I could tell that he really wanted me to come home for the summer. He visited me only once during my freshman year. I did go home for Christmas, but that was only a short vacation. Pop couldn't afford for me to fly home for every holiday or break. So I think—no, I know—he was really disappointed that I wouldn't be at home for the summer.

Cancer *of the* Spirit

The *Listen to Students Program* was the highlight of my first year at Prairie View. Being a part of it was a great way to end my freshman year. It was such a rewarding experience. I learned how I could develop and implement a program of my own. Of course, the focus of the program at Prairie View was quite different from the one I had in mind, but the essence of it was very similar—to assist young adults in overcoming whatever obstacles they face at vulnerable times in their lives.

At Prairie View, the challenges for students ranged from financial ones to doubts about having the brains to get through their course of study. The staff responsible for administering the program, and all the student counselors—two sophomores, three juniors, two seniors, and me—a mere freshman, were not only excellent workers, but also sympathetic to student concerns. All of us wanted to make sure that the *Listen to Students Program* would be around for many years to come. It was the one program that many students felt made a difference in their lives and one that they readily used. That's what really measured its success. I understand it's still going strong.

By the time I had completed my junior year at Prairie View, I knew I had chosen the right major. All of the courses I had taken seemed to be compatible with my future plans. Even those taught by professors that I didn't particularly like, were of great interest and, as I have found out since, of immense value to me. I worked with the *Listen to Students Program* every summer. It got better, and became more popular each year. During my senior year, I became a full-time worker.

Luckily for me and the other students, funding for the program was never in question. I now realize how valuable my undergraduate days at Prairie View really were, particularly the *Listen to Students Program*. It was a source of healing for me. It kept me from feeling sorry for myself by helping to keep my mind off Ma's death. That was the most important thing. The program also gave me the opportunity to look at myself and come to the realization that I have truly grown to like who I have become. It provided both spiritual and financial stability that helped me to gain more confidence in myself. The extra money I needed to fly home to see Pop from time to time was not an "issue." He finally got used to the idea that I was not coming home during the summer and began to like the program because, as he put it, "At least it pays your way home to see me."

By the beginning of my senior year at Prairie View, Pop had started seeing Ms. Ethel, a woman from the church who I've known all my life. She, Ma, and a few other women cooked many meals for church events over the years. Ms. Ethel has always seemed like such a kind and good-hearted lady. After Pop started dating her, when I would go home for breaks, he didn't seem to be as high-strung as he usually was. He even seemed to listen somewhat better. Praise the lord for Ms. Ethel!

At the end of my senior year, I had mixed feelings about graduating. Although I would be at Prairie View for two more years, getting my Masters degree from the School of Social Work, I felt a little sad about losing my undergrad classmates and being separated from the few very close friends I'd made during those four years. We, of course, promised to stay in touch, but I felt skeptical about that really happening. I'm glad, though, to say that we have.

Graduation day was wonderful; it was a bright, beautiful Texas day. And I was class valedictorian. Everyone had such a feeling of accomplishment. Pop walked with such pride, head held high and all. You would have thought he was the valedictorian. For the first time, I really knew how proud Pop was of me. He never said it, but I could tell. Pop and Ms. Ethel looked so good. They had arrived three days before because they wanted to spend a few days sightseeing and visiting with a friend of Ms. Ethel's. One of Pop's brothers and his family also came to my graduation. Pop was so happy to the point that his eyes welled up with tears. When I saw that, I couldn't control myself and broke down in tears, too.

The biggest surprise of that day was Teddy. Right out of high school, he had started working for a small advertising firm in Morristown. Four years later, he still loved the excitement of his job and was recently offered a position as assistant to the vice president. We had kept in touch by phone and letters, and had dated every time I went home. Even though we were so far apart, our feelings for one another had never changed. Still I was shocked that he showed up at my graduation. He told Pop not to tell me he was coming and had arrived the night before.

As I prepared my valedictory speech, I became more convinced than ever that I was meant to pursue my dream of setting up and directing a program for at-risk youth. The majority of my coursework over the four years was taken with that dream in mind. That was also my focal point in applying for admission to the School of Social Work. I was just as excited about my further studies and training, as I was about leaving home to attend college. I completed my graduate work in May of 1994.

Pop has accepted the fact that I will never live at home again. He sees how well I have done on my own. I'm also happy that he has done well on his own and now has someone in his life to share everything with. Neither of us will ever let go of our love for Ma. She will always remain in our hearts. We are doing the best we can, and it's all good — very good.

*   *   *   *   *   *

There is an eerie silence as Ama ends her story. Suddenly tears are streaming down her face. She rushes from the room with Marlana and Makeba following her. Understanding the memories and feelings that this gathering has evoked, the rest of the women sit silently until Hattie Mae says, "Say, is dare any mo of dat Harveys?" Leesha is the first to laugh out loud but is soon joined by all the others. Ena refills Hattie Mae's glass and all the others that are held out to her.

Ama, Marlana, and Makeba re-enter the room as Leesha makes a toast: "To our hostesses—here in the flesh and here in spirit," to which all the ladies say, "Hear, hear!" Ama, a little embarrassed, enthusiastically thanks everyone for being there. She says the get together, although heart-wrenching, had really, in some strange way, soothed her soul.

Suddenly she blurts out, "Let's have more 'Soothe Our Souls Sessions.' I know we can find a way to do it, even though we're from all over the place. This celebration was intended to be an upbeat occasion—and it has been—but I feel it's evolved into much, much more. Despite the fact that some parts of our lives have presented us with challenges that seemed overwhelming, we've all come through those times—mentally healthy and spiritually strong. Sharing your stories has given me some of your strength. I hope all of you feel that way, too. Am I right?" Everyone but Hattie Mae nods in agreement. "Then please don't let us end here. I know Ma is somewhere up there nodding her head in approval. This will be a weekend that I will never forget. I hope you won't either."

Cancer *of the* Spirit

" I sho enjoy myself dis weekend too," says Hattie Mae. " Cain't wait to see you chuirrun again. Gimme another Harveys, Ama."

Ama realizes that this celebration provided a secure and safe haven for everyone to comfortably get a lot of off their chests. She also has a strong feeling that this momentous weekend was just the first of many more to come.

*   *   *   *   *   *

Ife

January 10, 2004

Dearest Ama,

I hope all is well with you. I'm still in awe of your get together. It was a fantastic weekend! After several months of communication with you and several of the others regarding documenting our stories, I've finally accomplished that task. It was really a challenge to transcribe hours of conversation into ten separate stories, but I did it! It took longer than I expected, but was well worth the effort. Let me know if you like the way I pulled the stories together.

While documenting them, I discovered that I had forgotten quite a bit of what was said—even though it wasn't that long ago—and was happy to get the chance to hear everything again. That also helped me to set the scene so the stories and the comments were in the proper context. This labor of love has been one of my most rewarding experiences, especially since I have been interacting with the other women to be sure that I had accurately captured their stories. I'll be sending each lady a bound copy of the compiled narratives—like the one you received.

I have a surprise for you! Remember you suggested that we have more Soothe Our Souls sessions? Well, I've come up with a way to do it. The concern you had about everyone living all over the country has been taken care of. I had a really creative and talented sister develop a website—www.SootheOurSouls.com—that was launched on my birthday, January 6th. A bulletin board for discussions is one of the features of the website. Anyone can access it twenty-four hours a day. It's a place where we, and other women, can "meet" to talk about many of the issues that surfaced in the life stories we shared at the get together. Check out the site. You can send a message to me letting me know how you like it.

One last thing, Ama. In the spirit of our discussions and in honor of your mother, the website provides visitors the opportunity to give support to the Cancer Center at the Howard University Hospital.

I hope to hear from you soon. Let's stay in touch.

With affection,

Sharon

Afterwords

'Soothe Our Souls Sessions' will occur online 24/7, via the Soothe Our Souls Bulletin Board. You can become an active participant by choosing www.SootheOurSouls.com as your next web destination.

The Pass Code (four-digit number—a year) you'll need to access the character updates at Sootheoursouls.com is embedded in Hattie Mae's story. It is the year that PaPop moved his family to their own house on the farm—the Madison farm. The updates will provide revealing information about the exciting things that have happened to all ten women since the get together.

Finally, the identity of the character upon which the author's story is based is also revealed on the website. Click on the character updates link at SootheOurSouls.com

Cancer of the Spirit

ORDER FORM

To purchase Cancer of the Spirit, order online at www.SootheOurSouls.com or complete the following order form and send a money order to the address below.

Cancer of the Spirit   **(1 copy)** $21.95

Cancer of the Spirit   **(2 copies)** $40.00

Name: _____

Address: _____

_____

Phone Number: _____

E-mail Address: _____

Date of Order: _____

Order Information:

VIP Publishing, Inc.

9900 Greenbelt Road, Suite E 212

Lanham, MD 20706-2264

Ife@vippublishinginc.com

Inspirations in Indelible Ink!

THANKS FOR YOUR SUPPORT!!

SootheOurSouls.com

ORDER FORM

To purchase any of the following SootheOurSouls.com items, click on the website link to the store or complete the following order form, circle item(s) you want and send a money order to the address below.

Regular Tee Shirt . . . .$15.99 S/ M/ L/ XL

Baby Doll Tee Shirt . . . .$19.99 S/ M/ L/

Infant/Toddler Tee Shirt . . . .$9.99 I/T

Journal $9.99

Large Mug $13.99

Regular Mug $11.99

Coasters . . . .$ 4.99

Wooden (Coaster) Box $18.99

Mouse Pad $11.99

Wall Clock $12.99

White Teddy Bear $14.99

Tote Bag $14.99

Oval Stickers $2.99

Note: MD residents, add 5% tax

Name: _____

Address: _____

Phone Number: (optional) _____

E-mail Address: _____

Date of Order: _____ Tee Shirt Size:_____

Contact Information:
Carole 'Ife' Keene
Chief Executive Officer
Soothe Our Souls
9900 Greenbelt Road, Suite E 212
Lanham, MD 20706-2264
Email: Ife@SoothOurSouls.com

Note: Prices subject to change.

THANKS FOR YOUR SUPPORT!!

Herman and Annie Kilgore, my late uncle and aunt, who loved and supported me through the decades, set an example of love, faith and commitment that continues to inspire me.